Understanding the Power and Politics of Public Education

Understanding the Power and Politics of Public Education

Implementing Policies to Achieve Equal Opportunity for All

Janet D. Mulvey and Bruce S. Cooper

ROWMAN & LITTLEFIELD
Lanham • Boulder • New York • London

Published by Rowman & Littlefield
A wholly owned subsidiary of The Rowman & Littlefield Publishing Group, Inc.
4501 Forbes Boulevard, Suite 200, Lanham, Maryland 20706
www.rowman.com

Unit A, Whitacre Mews, 26-34 Stannary Street, London SE11 4AB

Copyright © 2016 by Janet D. Mulvey and Bruce S. Cooper

All rights reserved. No part of this book may be reproduced in any form or by any electronic or mechanical means, including information storage and retrieval systems, without written permission from the publisher, except by a reviewer who may quote passages in a review.

British Library Cataloguing in Publication Information Available

Library of Congress Cataloging-in-Publication Data

Names: Mulvey, Janet D., author. | Cooper, Bruce S., author.
Title: Understanding the power and politics of public education : implementing policies to achieve equal opportunity for all / Janet D. Mulvey and Bruce S. Cooper.
Description: Lanham : Rowman & Littlefield [2016] | Includes bibliographical references and index.
Identifiers: LCCN 2016017171 (print) | LCCN 2016025324 (ebook) |
 ISBN 9781475820874 (cloth : alk. paper) | ISBN 9781475820881 (pbk. : alk. paper) |
 ISBN 9781475820898 (Electronic)
Subjects: LCSH: Public schools—United States. | Educational equalization—United States.
Classification: LCC LA217.2 .M84 2016 (print) | LCC LA217.2 (ebook) |
 DDC 371.010973—dc23
LC record available at https://lccn.loc.gov/2016017171

∞™ The paper used in this publication meets the minimum requirements of American National Standard for Information Sciences—Permanence of Paper for Printed Library Materials, ANSI/NISO Z39.48-1992.

Printed in the United States of America

Contents

Foreword	vii
Introduction	ix
PART I: STORIES OF EDUCATION'S POWER	**1**
1 Change through Educational Opportunity	3
2 Cognitive Functioning and Poverty	13
3 How Early Is Early Enough?	25
PART II: SUCCESS AND FAILURE	**39**
4 Failure for the Masses	41
5 The Reality of Poverty and Neglect	51
PART III: SUMMARY OF U.S. AND INTERNATIONAL EFFORTS TO INCREASE EDUCATIONAL OPPORTUNITY AND MOBILITY	**67**
6 Changing the Landscape: Reinventing Public Education	69
7 Educating Communities	81
8 Intergenerational Influences: The Power of Education on Children's Lives	91
9 Summary and Future Implications	105
Index	123
About the Authors	129

Foreword
Carlos R. McCray

Janet D. Mulvey and Bruce S. Cooper show again in this book just how important and critical education is for families and their children, everywhere and under different circumstances. As with their first book, *Intersecting Children's Health, Education and Welfare* (2012), this new book links the three critical variables of income, health, and education to show just how important education is to children: their learning, opportunities, good health, and economic futures in the twenty-first century.

While the first book hooked together ("intersected") children's health, their education, and their welfare (based on income), this book analyzes the key variables in the troika of *education,* concentrating on the three *P*s (power, politics, and policy) in society's changing and improving schooling for all. This new Mulvey-Cooper book explores and explains the "power" of education, adding two *P*s (policies and programs and patience and persistence), based on the activities and politics of setting and implementing policies to benefit all children in schools and in life.

This process is hardly easy, for it requires schools and the education system to be central to relieving the "poverty" conditions of families; and in so doing, to enable children to get good, quality education and better health care and then quality jobs and higher income. Other nations have been more instrumental in providing nationalized health care, free preschool, and equality in both teacher preparation and placement for all schools.

As in England, for example, private schools can be expensive and somewhat exclusive, but health care is readily available and at lower costs or free to all in the United Kingdom. In the United States, poor families may have to stand on lines in a clinic or emergency room (ER) to get treatments or none, a serious problem for those without health insurance, usually associated with a good job. And it begins prenatal in life.

The authors point out the importance of early life experiences that set the stage for school and later life success. They discuss the damage done by polluted environments, poor nutrition, family stress, and neighborhood violence. Brain and cognitive development are explained as they relate to socioeconomic conditions. Research-based evidence is provided showing the results of impoverishment from the lack of preventative care while in utero to the age of five.

The demographic shift in public schools—where current and future enrollments have become a more diverse minority—calls for teacher preparation that is very different from the traditional programs in colleges and universities. So this book not only identifies the problems of health and education, as related to income and wealth, but also discusses how to break these conditions, and thus to make education less dependent on income or race, or language, and more equitable based on a full effort to improved education for all.

The book is divided into three sections. Part I reinforces the "power of education," as a means for improving children's lives, families, work, and health. Part II elaborates on the effects on good education on the community and the "masses," and discusses the "reality" of what happens when a society neglects education and learning for the poor.

In part III, the book examines the long-term effects of poverty, poor education, and poor health. Not a good or happy combination. Finally, the book makes strong suggestions for improving the education for children, their lives, their communities, and their futures. And we recognize the importance and struggles of ending racism through Nelson Mandela, who said, "Education is the most powerful weapon which you can use to change the world."

Education is thus a critical activity in every society: from preparing the next generation to have healthy lives, access to opportunity for employment, and the ability to raise a family in a safe, healthy, and nurturing environment.

Introduction
Janet D. Mulvey and Bruce S. Cooper

Education offers essential, available opportunities for social mobility, success, and influence in life. Deprived of education, people are often relegated to lower societal status, economic limits, personal illness—and possible despair (see Mulvey & Cooper, 2012). The power of knowing "how to" and to engage in learning develops the individual and motivates his or her contribution to the community. In our stories here, we reflect on the words of Namita Patil (2012): "Education can be used as a tool to empower the individual. Through child-centered learning, students are able to see their own role in transformation. Societal change comes from the collective transformation of individuals within that society" (p. 205).

New policies and laws, however, have placed public education in peril. Charter schools and vouchers that allow tax dollars to be used for private and religious schools, added to constitutional amendments that disallow race to be a factor in school demographics, have resulted in resegregation. Tax dollars taken away from the public schools have defunded and underresourced schools in low socioeconomic areas. Reducing the quality of public education in poor neighborhoods has resulted in diminished opportunities for millions of our youth.

Living in poverty, being oppressed, and lacking education too often resulted in diminished social mobility for individuals, groups, and communities. A quality education can change those who are impoverished or oppressed to become successful contributors for themselves, their families, and society. Opportunity for quality schooling benefits everyone and can alter the direction, both socially and economically, for entire regions and countries.

Famous historic individuals born under poor economic conditions have become some of our most admired leaders: Benjamin Franklin, Abraham Lincoln, and Henry Ford are perhaps those best known. More recent examples include former President William Clinton and Supreme Court Justice Sonia Sotomayor. Although living in poor environments, the education they received helped both individuals rise to positions of power and influence. Unfortunately, they are exceptions to the rule; most individuals living in low socioeconomic environments are relegated to remain without such promise.

Current policies regarding public education are painfully reminiscent of the days prior to the 1950s when "separate but unequal" was the accepted rule for much of the populace. Using tax dollars to support private and charter schools reduces funding for public schools, and the 2007 ruling of the US Supreme Court have reversed racial representation in schools across the country. Today schools have become as racially and socioeconomically segregated as they were in the mid-twentieth century.

This book examines and reports on the *power of education* as the change agent for individuals, communities, and societies. It follows the policies and politics that have affected quality, efficiency, and opportunity for Americans above and below the poverty line. Case studies look into the influence of education on individual persons, or communities, here in the United States and abroad. Individual stories look at extremes of oppression and purposeful invisibility of needs by policy makers and government. We encourage those within learning institutions, policy making agencies, and those holding political positions to examine the benefits of education for our country now and in future generations.

For example, on December 6, 2011, President Barack Obama spoke about the inequalities existing for those living in America:

> This kind of gaping inequality gives lie to the promise that's at the very heart of America: that this is a place where you can make it if you try. We tell people—we tell our kids—that in this country, even if you're born with nothing, work hard and you can get into the middle class. We tell them, your children will have a chance to do even better than you do. That's why immigrants from all over the world historically have flocked to our shores. (Speech delivered at Osawatomie High School in Kansas, December 6, 2011)

Conditions of impoverishment are researched and related to educational opportunity for mobility, as well as the impact for individuals whom education has helped and for those who have been ignored. The change in demographics is examined in our public schools as well as the need to assure quality education to further our democratic government.

We implore policy makers and politicians to look to the future of the country instead of focusing simply on agendas for reelection. The population demographic projections for 2050 are predicting a vast shift, and the increase for the United States will come mainly from immigrants. Passel and Cohn (2008) project that "if current trends continue, the population of the United States will rise to 438 million in 2050 . . . and 82% of the increase will be due to immigrants and their U.S. born descendants" (p. 1).

Education for the masses is critical to maintain a democratic system, a sustainable gross national product (GNP), and a competitive edge in the global marketplace. Quality public education is a must to assure equal opportunity for all socioeconomic levels and provide incentive to develop marketable skills in an advanced society.

Compelling stories from Africa, Asia, and the Americas show just how education in various cultures and regions of the world are the force for (1) not only survival, but also (2) upward mobility and (3) social contribution. Immigration issues for those both legal and illegal can contribute to abject poverty and perpetuate generations of impoverishment and despair are examined. Hope for understanding the absolute necessities of an educated populace for societal survival is a large objective of the research, personal stories, and scientific theory imbedded in this book.

Economic prosperity is an absolute necessity for nations to remain competitive, to assure a healthy workforce, a satisfied populace involved in assuring democratic rights, and a force for peace internationally. Quality education for all is the only avenue to eradicate poverty, develop a skilled workforce, and benefit individuals, families, communities, and societies.

Political agendas must unite around policies for an educated populace if we are to remain an influential force worldwide. Our strength as a nation depends upon shared decision making, focused on the good of the people, not the special interests of the few. Remember, "If a man empties his purse into his head, no man can take it away from him. An investment in knowledge always pays the best interest" (Benjamin Franklin).

REFERENCES

Mulvey, J., & Cooper, B. S. (2012). *Intersections of children's health, education and welfare*. New York: Palgrave MacMillan.

Obama, B. (2011). Obama in Kansas slams Republicans over inequality. http://www.bbc.com/news/world-us-canada-16061185.

Passel, J., & Cohn, V. (2008). *U.S. population projections: 2005–2050*. Pew Research Center, February 11.

Patil, N. (2012, Jan-Feb-Mar). Role of education social change. *International Educational E-Journal*, *1*(2), 205–210. http://www.oiirj.org/ejournal/Jan-Feb-Mar2012IEEJ/38.pdf.

KEY QUESTIONS

1. How can we educate policy makers on all levels of government to rely on scientific research to provide and assure equal opportunity for an education leading to economic and social mobility?
2. What are the factors for cognitive growth?
3. How can we guarantee preventative measures and prepare children's readiness to learn?

    Medically
    Environmentally
    Economically
    Nutritionally

4. How early is early enough?

    Prenatal
    Understanding the development of the brain
    Language acquisition
    Developmental readiness
    Educating parents and future parents on early developmental needs

5. How have our public schools changed over the years?

    Demographically
    Linguistically
    Culturally

6. How should we adapt and change education to meet the new population?
7. How do we use developmental readiness factors to teach?

    Assessments for formative learning
    Authentic assessments
    Standardized testing

8. How should we educate teachers at colleges and universities?

    How can we professionalize the teaching career?
    How can we begin preparing teachers for twenty-first-century knowledge and skills?

9. How can we succeed in educating the masses?
10. How can we improve intergenerational experiences?
11. What type of citizenry is required to maintain a sound democracy?

Part I

STORIES OF EDUCATION'S POWER

Chapter 1

Change through Educational Opportunity

Janet D. Mulvey

In 1897, Emile Durkheim, a French sociologist, argued against the transformative power of education when he posited, "Education can be reformed only if society itself is reformed—education is only the reflection of society. It imitates and reproduces the latter—it does not create it (1897/1951, pp. 372–373).

We also assert that although societies are sectioned and divided according to wealth and power, the only opportunity to join influence with the privileged is to gain knowledge, skills, and self-awareness of one's voice and determination. If we succumb to the current inadequacies and inequalities in education, we give up equal rights as individuals in the society where we reside. Bowles and Gintis (1976) saw and reported on the inequities that still exist today in public education: "It is a society where no one feels obligated to pay taxes for the broader social good and where welfare 'reform' means denying benefits to children if their parents cannot find work . . . [a] society where those who do not fit in are shunned" (p. 85).

Equal opportunity is measured not only by the amount of dollars given to a school, but also by the much-argued policy and classroom level of per-pupil expenditures (see Cooper & Speakman, 2003). We need to recognize that living conditions outside the school environment can account for much of the students' inability to enter the classroom cognitively ready to learn. Improving educational growth—learning—access may only be accomplished by changing the climate in which too many children live and giving them the power to improve their lives.

Renate Nestvogel wrote stories in *School Education in "Third World" Countries: Dream or Trauma?* about young girls in Pakistan who have primary responsibilities in the home and cannot afford the obligatory school uniforms to attend their local government schools. Children as young as four years of age already have responsibilities in the fields or in the home, making an education secondary to their survival (2012, pp. 205–214).

Children living in poverty worldwide, even those who gain access to education, are often thwarted by the extreme necessities of survival: food, clothing, and shelter. Here in the United States, for example, an estimated forty-eight million students suffer these disadvantages, including sixteen million children who do not get enough food on a daily basis. How can we address these issues and convince those who hold economic power to realize or care about the lost potential of this increasingly large sector of society? What loss would we have seen, for example, if J. K. Rowling of *Harry Potter* fame remained on the streets, unrecognized for her talents?

Societies, here in the United States and abroad, are organized into narrow bands of identification, including successful business, corporate, and professional strata or labor, and lower-skill-level competencies. Those with higher economic assignations are treated to climates of educational expectations rich with resources and opportunity. Those on the lower rungs of identification have fewer expectations and exist in overcrowded classrooms, with less experienced teachers and fewer resources. Singer and Pezone (2003) identify such conditions when they wrote:

> Under the circumstances, it is not surprising that our school system is designed to sort children out and leave many uneducated. To legitimize the way our society is organized, its schools teach competitive behavior and social inequality as if they were fundamental law of nature. Just as with the economy, some are rewarded in school, others are punished, and both groups are taught that rewards and punishment are the result of their own efforts (Kohn, 1999). (p. np)

Historically, immigrants coming to the United States, Great Britain, and other European countries enter with the hope of better lives, quality education for their children, and freedom from oppression. For too many, however, these hopes quickly die as their needs to be educated and economically stable are ignored. The lack of opportunity becomes an entrapment into frustration and self-deprecation. Paulo Freire wrote back in 1968:

> Self-deprecation is a characteristic of the oppressed, which derives from their internalization of the opinion of the oppressor—so often do they hear that they are good for nothing—that they know nothing, are incapable of learning anything, that they are lazy and unproductive—that in the end they become convinced of their own unfitness. (p. 63)

This perception can and must be changed if we are to continue as a democracy in this country and see peace abroad. We must alter the mind-set and political direction to become a psychology for success; and the place for that change resides in free public and government-supported schools. How can we deny the inequity in our schools, providing opportunity for one group and denying it in the other?

Recent statistical analysis by the Education for All (EFA) in December 2013 showed that poverty is diminished through education and skills training. According to Winthrop et al. (2013)

> There is, in fact, a significant return on investment in education. . . . Modest early-stage investments to ensure that each child attends school, remains in school, and learns in school can yield significant economic return. (p. 2)

The cost of educational spending, now, has large payoffs for individuals, families, communities, and society at large in future years. The effects of poverty on the individual are described by Paulo Freire, as he and his family slipped from the middle class into sharing the life of the "wretched of the earth" (1968, p. 30).

Projections for a population explosion (Passel & Cohn, reporting in Pew Hispanic Center, 2008) demand a more effective public education system for all, founded on new skills for twenty-first-century living. Program resources for the technological advances that are yet to come and the critical thinking necessary to keep pace with an exponentially growing computer information science society must be allocated throughout the public education system.

PAOLO FREIRE'S CHANGE FOR SOCIETY

The inspiration for Freire's educational philosophy was his own personal experience in feeling the effects of poverty and despair. Being hungry, becoming unmotivated in school, and watching the fear and frustration of his parents, Freire, at age eleven, became determined to change the direction of his life and to assure that other children did not suffer the same fate. As he observed and studied his environment, he came to realize "that their ignorance and lethargy were the direct product of the whole situation of economic, social and political domination—and of paternalism—of which they are victims" (1968, p. 30).

Freire's experience in his early life, and determination to bring change, ended with his imprisonment in Brazil, during the junta revolution in 1964. Escaping to Chile, where he remained exiled for several years, he began developing a progressive educational philosophy. Targeting the poor and oppressed, Freire posited that by giving the students the ability to attain knowledge and skills, and think critically, they would be able to participate in their own self-determination.

His works have inspired critical thought and action for individuals to examine the lack of social justice inherent in societal structures. In Freire's own words,

No system of education is neutral. Bias is inherent in any selection and ordering of facts. . . . Any appraisal of the prospects of democratic education through literacy, a literacy that reads both the word and world must start from an articulated standpoint, on expressed terrain. Just what is the current situation? What should be done about it? (p. 78)

LEARNING FROM HISTORY: PEACE vs. CHAOS

Public education for all in the United States was advocated and championed by Horace Mann, often called the father of the American "Common School." Prior to his position as secretary of the Massachusetts Board of Education, schooling was private and tuition was paid for by the more economically well off. It was his contention that to maintain a stable and peaceful democracy, the citizenry needed basic literacy skills to become informed about public policy and ideals. He declared, "Without undervaluing any other human agency, it may be safely affirmed that the Common School . . . may become the most effective and benignant of all forces of civilization" (*New York Times*, 1953).

Correlation studies have examined the connection between countries' education policies and types of existing government. The more educated the populace, the more democratic the government.

The Common Schools in the United States began the tax-paid education policy, enabling all children to attend primary school without personal cost. The results are the public schools still in effect today. But did Mann mean that tax and funding would be more beneficial to the affluent? Or did he believe that all should receive quality and equitable resources? Horace Mann began the process for education for all, which historically has morphed into a battle to provide quality for all.

John Dewey agreed and supported the contentions of Horace Mann and pushed for quality education to be equitable among the masses. Dewey called for intellectual stimulation through development of community within the classroom. According to Dewey, "When the school introduces and trains each child of society into membership within such a little community, saturating him with the spirit of service, . . . we shall have the . . . best guarantee of a larger society which is worthy, lovely and harmonious" (Dewey, 1907, p. 196).

Countries that provide public education to their children, while inequitable in many ways, experience more participation from the populace in government affairs, hear more voice in public policies, and create greater feelings of security within the environment. Countries that deny education to large parts of their population, based on religious beliefs, gender, and wealth, too often are in states of turmoil or revolution.

The United States still struggles to deliver quality education to the students in poorer communities but affords awards to those already rich in resources. Comparing performance with other democratic countries finds us well behind and dropping in proficiency in literacy, math, and science. If we compare poverty to educational attainment, we can see not just the effect of the poverty, but the diminished quality of education dispensed to those without socioeconomic means.

The following graphs depict educational quality versus socioeconomic means. The chart in figure 1.1 displays the ratio of low socioeconomic status (SES) students more likely to be lower achievers in comparison to students with higher SES. For example, in Portugal a student with low SES is three times as likely to be a low achiever in mathematics as a student with high SES. The United States student with low SES is almost four times as likely to be a low achiever as one with high SES.

According to the Organisation for Economic Co-operation and Development (OECD, 2006), 15 percent of American test score variation on international assessment can be explained by socioeconomic differences. But the United States has lower than average resiliency rate (25 percent) than other students who are economically disadvantaged from countries participating on the international performance tests. And some questions appear regarding

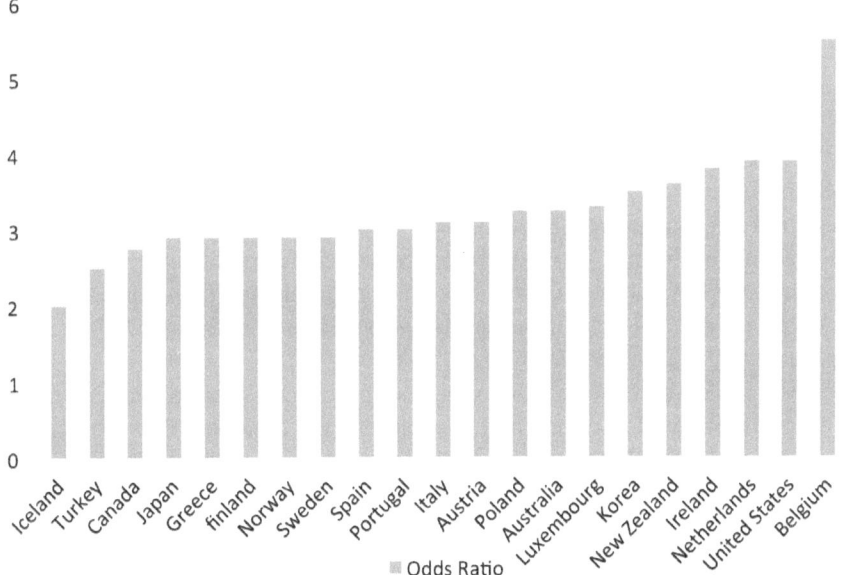

Figure 1.1 **Likelihood of Students with the Lowest SES to Be Lowest Performers when Compared to Students with High SES.** *Source*: Education at a Glance 2006: OECD Indicators, Paris.

the reaction to the tests, "A 2011 study found that PISA scores are an economic indicator: rising scores are a good sign that a country's economy will grow as well" (Khaopa, 2011). Social adaptation, acceptance, and change are important aspects of educational acquisition. Students living in impoverished or oppressed circumstances can only evaluate their own surroundings through the enlightenment brought by literacy, technology, and by attending the institution called school. As Patil (2012) explains:

> Education is directly related to the development of an individual and the community. It is the most important single factor for economic development as well as social emancipation. For weaker sections of society have a special significance because . . . illiteracy and social backwardness has been used for harassment, humiliation and economic exploitation. (pp. 207–208)

Personal stories reflect the power of education to change or provide opportunities to those who have found a way to overcome adversity caused by poverty and oppressed environments. The stories are combined with research and statistical data on the rewards, successes, and failures of educational policies locally and internationally. We question, how can the facts be ignored? What can we learn from those who have persevered? Can we remediate current policy and include the have-nots with the haves? Altering our current focus on education to consider the future of our country is not only desired but a must!

EDUCATION AS ESCAPE FROM POVERTY

After the 2014 Super Bowl, Richard Sherman, the quarterback for the Seattle Seahawks, came into the news for his outburst and "trash talk" that occurred after the playoff game against the New England Patriots. Why was this event significant? While admonished and criticized for unsportsmanlike conduct, we have come to know how this accomplished player became successful, not only as an athlete but also as a scholar and Stanford University graduate.

Born in Watts, one of the toughest neighborhoods in Los Angeles, California, Richard Sherman had to overcome the dominant characteristic of student apathy for learning and education inherent in this poverty stricken area. The Compton schools in Los Angeles, which he attended, had a graduation rate of 57 percent, not taking into account the number of unreported dropouts. Taking advantage of sports as a distraction from a gang-infested area, he used school to participate in his natural athletic abilities and found academics as a result. He excelled in school, taking AP courses that resulted in admission to Stanford University.

Sherman played football at Stanford, was drafted into the pro-football league, and has excelled as an athlete. He was also a successful student at Stanford and was realistic in his ambitions. He returns to his old neighborhood and uses his fame and status to inspire young students to stay in school and realize their dreams. Graduating from Stanford in 2010 with a degree in communications, he is pursuing a master's degree and planning for the next stage of his life.

Richard Sherman was able to escape life in an urban area rife with poverty and despair. Sherman, in fact, used athletics and education as a driving force to escape the too common troubled life styles in poor neighborhoods. Now he is giving back to try to make education the change agent collectively in areas where youth role models are few and far between. Meeting the needs of each individual kid results in meeting the needs of the society. Our total social system, economically and politically, relies on the collective intelligence of the populace.

Sonia Sotomayor, Supreme Court Justice, credits her extended family and education for success as a lawyer, judge, Supreme Court Justice. In her autobiography she writes: "I came to accept—that many of the gaps in my knowledge and understanding were limits of class and cultural background, not the lack of aptitude or application as I feared" (2013, p. 135). Sotomayor goes on to discuss how she often felt out of place, different, and less accepted in her postsecondary education.

Her unwillingness to accept the status quo for poor and Puerto Rican migrants has helped bring to light the unequal opportunity for poor and immigrant families. Education for the nation depends on the understanding of support systems from family, local communities, government, and schools. Mobility is directly correlated to the knowledge gained through good education.

Sotomayor's and Sherman's stories—like J. K. Rowling's and others—while inspirational, invite political comments, "If they can do it, so should all others." The myth of work hard and you will succeed has become increasingly more difficult. As a matter of fact, many on the lower socioeconomic spectrum work very hard—two or three jobs just to stay afloat while those in the upper quartile have access to good schools, postsecondary education, and potential for higher paying jobs.

According to Reeves (2014), "Lack of upward mobility is souring the national mood. It is that America is failing to live up to American equalitarian principles, measured by the promise of equal opportunity for all, the idea that every child born into poverty can rise to the top" (p. np).

Researchers, educators, and theorists all agree: knowledge is power. It strengthens an understanding of current conditions within a societal structure, activates the populace for change, and develops a stronger desire to participate in political processes. Human capital is the strength of any and all countries, and education is the catalyst for growth and prosperity for all.

The United States offers free education for all children but it has regressed back to the days of separate and unequal. Children who live in poverty attend substandard schools that have fewer resources and fewer successes. We need to look at the causes, remove the obstacles, and solve the problems to eradicate the perpetuation of generations living at or below the poverty line.

As Nelson Mandela (2013) said: "A good head and good heart are always a formidable combination. But when you add to that a literate tongue or pen, then you have something very special."

SUMMARY

History has set the stage for education's purpose and necessity. The Founding Fathers looked upon education as the only way to preserve a democratic and free society. Public education for the masses allows all citizens the opportunity to become informed about issues of the country and to participate in their choice for a government "for the people."

The current policies and political stance for public education have been remiss in providing the equal access for all. Those who live in impoverished areas receive a lesser quality in their schools. Funding is dispersed among the charter schools and other private institutions, taking away needed money for quality public education.

Inspirational stories should be catalysts to recognize the possibilities of freeing our youth from the confines of poverty and lifting them toward productive citizenry. The supports from the school and members of society freed from restrictive policies can change the trends from failure to success.

It is time for policy makers and politicians to examine the detriment to the public education sector of their policies of funding and general support. Horace Mann in 1830 understood the power of education for the masses. He believed that the strength of our country relied upon the "intelligence and virtue" of the people. And he insisted, "If we do not prepare children to become good citizens . . . then our republic must go down to destruction" (*New York Times*, 1953).

REFERENCES

Bowles, S., & Gintis, H. (1976). *Schooling in capitalistic America: Educational reform and the contradictions of economic life.* New York: Basic Books.

Cooper, B. S., & Speakman, J. T., eds. (2003). *Optimizing educational resources (advances in educational productivity)*. Bingley, UK: Emerald Publishing Group.

Dewey, J. (1907). *The school and society*. Chicago: University of Chicago Press.

Durkheim, E. (1897/1951). *Suicide: A study in sociology*. New York: Free Press, pp. 372–373.

Freire, P. (1968/70). *Pedagogy of the oppressed*. New York: Bloomsbury Publishing.

Khaopa, W. (2011). PISA scores "a good indicator of future economic growth." *The Nation*. www.nationmultimedia.com/2011/06/27/national/PISA-scores-a-good-indicator-of-future-economic-gr-30158765.html.

Mandela, N., cited in Strauss, V. (2013). Nelson Mandela on the power of education. *The Washington Post*. https://washingtonpost.com/news/answer-sheet/wp/2013/12/05/nelson-mandelas-famous-quote-on-education/.

New York Times. (1953, September 15). Education report: Horace Mann.

Nestvogel, R. (2012). *School education in "third world" countries: Dream or trauma?* https://www.waxman.com/fileadmin/media/zusatext/postlethwaite/nestvogel.pdf.

OECD. (2006). *Education at a Glance 2006: OECD Indictors*. Paris.

Passel, J. S. & Cohn, D. V. (2008). *U.S. population projections*. Washington, DC: Pew Hispanic Center.

Reeves, R. (2014, August 20). Equal opportunity, and the American dream. *National Journal*. www.nationaljournal.com/2014/08/20/equal-opportunity-and-american-dream.

Singer, A., & Pezone, M. (2003, July). Education for social change: From theory to practice. *Workplace*, 5(2), p. np.

Sotomayor, S. (2013). *My beloved world*. New York: Random House.

Winthrop, R., Bulloch, G., Bhatt, P., & Wood, A. (2013). *Investment in global education: Strategic imperative for business*. Brooking Institute (September), pp. 1–44.

Chapter 2

Cognitive Functioning and Poverty

Vibha K. Solanki

The United States has become more interested and focused on our international ranking on the PISA (Programme for International Students Assessment). The BBC (2015) reported on the top forty nations in reading and math. The United States ranked twenty-third in reading and thirty-sixth in math, placing the nation below the fiftieth percentile of nations reported.

Schools have been mandated to increase and improve instruction in measured content areas and enforce standardized assessments to gauge outcomes. If we ignore socioeconomic readiness and environmental factors, all students have been placed in a one-size-fits-all curricula according to age-designated grade levels. This chapter focuses on how we can increase the power of educational possibilities by improving the environments in poor communities.

What specifically can and should local schools do to help their students, regardless of location, SES, opportunity, and other problems? Mulvey and Cooper (2012) attempted to show how being poor affects children's health and education, which in turn limit each other. Poor children are less likely to be healthy and have access to a good education. What can we do to improve all three forces, making children feel, operate, and learn better?

Many of the poorest of the children who come to our schools have spent no time at all in school-like settings during the first five years of their life. Some school-age children spend only about thirty of their waking hours a week in schools, and then for only about two-thirds of the weeks in a year. In the course of a full year, students might spend just under a thousand hours in school, and almost five times that amount of time in their neighborhood and with their families (Berliner, 2006). Berliner indicates that for all children those five thousand hours require learning to be a member of one or more cultural groups in that community, learning to behave appropriately in diverse settings, learning ways to get along with others, to fix things, to think, and to explain things to others. These are natural and influential experiences in growing up; but for poor children, what is learned in those settings can be harmful and antiestablishment.

Many of the families in impoverished neighborhoods are so poorly equipped to raise healthy children that even the schools those children attend would have a hard time educating them, even if these schools were professionally organized and run (Berliner, 2006).

Cognitive development beginning in infancy is the process of intellectual growth, associated with the ability to reason, problem solve, process, and apply in relation to developmental learning. Better cognitive development leads to better brain functions, allowing a person to perform more challenging tasks that can lead to being more successful in different areas of his or her life.

Regardless of the age of the child, research shows that children who grow up in poverty are more likely to have lower levels of cognitive development, which leads to poorer academic performance. The longer the child is exposed to impoverished conditions, the worse his or her cognitive development and abilities will be. The longer the child is subjected to negative stimuli, the more likely the child is likely to suffer harm. When children are not able adequately to learn, they will not be able to learn how to better themselves, which can include not being able to learn how to function at a job.

Those who live in poverty have been shown to face emotional and social challenges, acute and chronic stressors, cognitive lags, and health and safety issues. Children who are raised in poverty behave differently from those who are not; these obstacles affect academic and social success (Edwards, 2012). Students whose families are poor may "act out," be impatient and impulsive, and show less empathy for others. Impoverished children may be subject to health and safety issues such as malnutrition, dangers in the home, and insufficient health care. This may lead to more absences from school, tardiness, and undiagnosed illnesses and disabilities, which may hinder their learning process (Edwards, 2012). Edwards explains that schools in high-poverty areas are given less funding than schools that already thrive in wealth.

Furthermore, these schools are more likely to have teachers who teach subjects that are outside of their concentration; thus, when students are given standardized tests, data demonstrate a correlation between poverty and low cognitive achievement. Edwards (2012) explains that poor achievement relates to self-esteem; students with low expectations set themselves up for very little success in life.

Pervasive environmental factors affect children in their physiological, emotional, and cognitive development (Marston, 2013). Marston explains, "Data collected from the 1997–2008 National Health Interview Surveys found that family income below the federal poverty level were associated with higher levels of developmental, learning and intellectual disabilities"

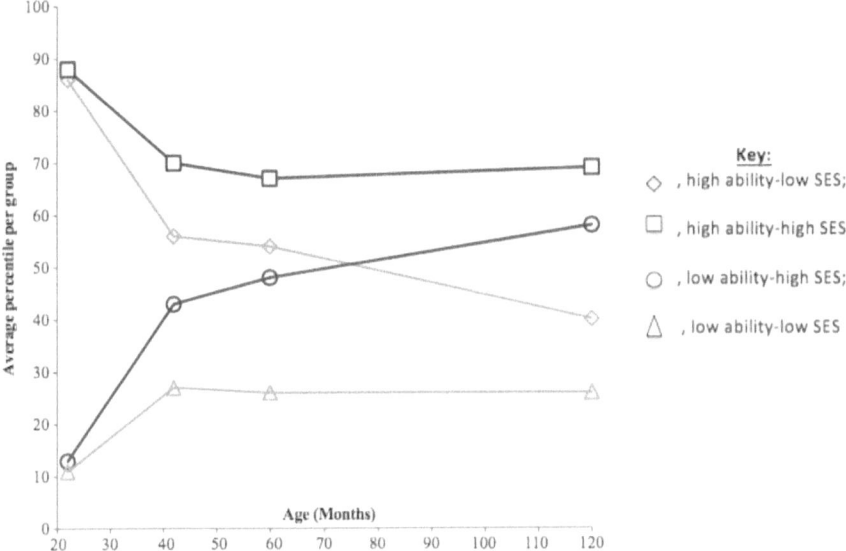

Figure 2.1 Development of High and Low Ability Children by Socioeconomic Group.
Source: Jerrim & Vignoles, 2013, p. 888.

(p. np). In a recent media campaign (September/October 2014), New York TV channels bought to light that thousands of children (143,000) in New York City were unable neither to read nor write. We have to ask ourselves: is this the fault of the public school system or is the problem deeper?

Children from disadvantaged backgrounds have poorer cognitive skills than their more advantaged peers, and such differences are apparent from a very early age (Jerim & Vignoles, 2013): "Initially able children from disadvantaged backgrounds quickly lose ground in terms of their cognitive skills to their rich but less able peers" (p. 887).

At the first time point in figure 2.1, twenty-two months, both high ability–high SES and high ability–low SES children are at the same point, roughly the 88th percentile of the achievement distribution. But by the time of the second assessment, taken at 42 months, the latter group slip to the 55th percentile, and, at the final point, 120 months, slips further to the 40th percentile. In contrast, high ability children from advantaged homes remain much higher up in the test score distribution, above the 70th percentile through to 120 months. Even more strikingly, low ability children from advantaged homes have moved up from the 12th to the 60th percentile over the same period.

The conclusion that can be made is that initially able children from poor backgrounds are overtaken in terms of their cognitive skill by low ability–high SES children before they begin a secondary education

(Jerim & Vignoles, 2013). The authors indicate that by the age of five, smart children from poorer backgrounds have been overtaken by less smart children from richer ones; from this point on, the gaps tend to widen farther.

Education is a key component affecting the well-being of the poor (Lam, 2014). Both home and school environments play significant roles in promoting or hampering cognitive skill development over time. From the outset, disadvantaged children's opportunities to learn are limited by the relationships among their backgrounds, contexts, enrollment, progression, and completion of schooling (Rolleston, 2014). As Rolleston highlights, a key early indicator of reduced opportunities to learn for disadvantaged children is delayed initial enrollment in schooling, while differences in opportunities go back farther, to preschooling and early childhood.

While the benefits of education are not reducible to the development of measurable skills, many important productive abilities are rooted in cognitive skills, in whose development formal schooling plays a fundamental role (Rolleston, 2014). Primary and lower secondary schooling plays a particularly important role in the development of basic cognitive skills, especially literacy and numeracy, and these skills in turn form the foundation for the development of more complex cognitive skills, such as problem-solving skills (Rolleston, 2014). The author suggests that "skills developed through education may improve young people's prospects of entering the labor market and enable them to adapt better to the rapidly changing demands of the economy" (p. 135).

In contexts where home disadvantage threatens to undermine the development of children's cognitive skills, school environments represent what is typically the largest influence on children outside their homes. Rolleston indicates that schools are arguably more accessible and efficient sites for intervention. Disadvantage is a major source of gaps in cognitive skills between the poor and the affluent groups: improving timely enrollment has been shown to be a crucial first base in equalizing educational opportunity. Strong links between early enrollment is almost universal, and weakening the link, for example between household wealth and learning, is a significant equity challenge that requires specific attention to quality schooling for the poorest (Rolleston, 2014).

Learning opportunities are vital to children as they develop cognitive ability and interpersonal skills through a wide gamut of learning experiences. The absence of such opportunities may hinder children's intellectual development and ability to cope with other people (see figure 2.2), thus negatively impacting their interpersonal growth (Lam, 2014). Poverty-stricken families are typically circumscribed by a variety of life-stressing events such as economic hardship. Suffering from prolonged distress may initiate maladaptive functioning and negative response (Lam, 2014).

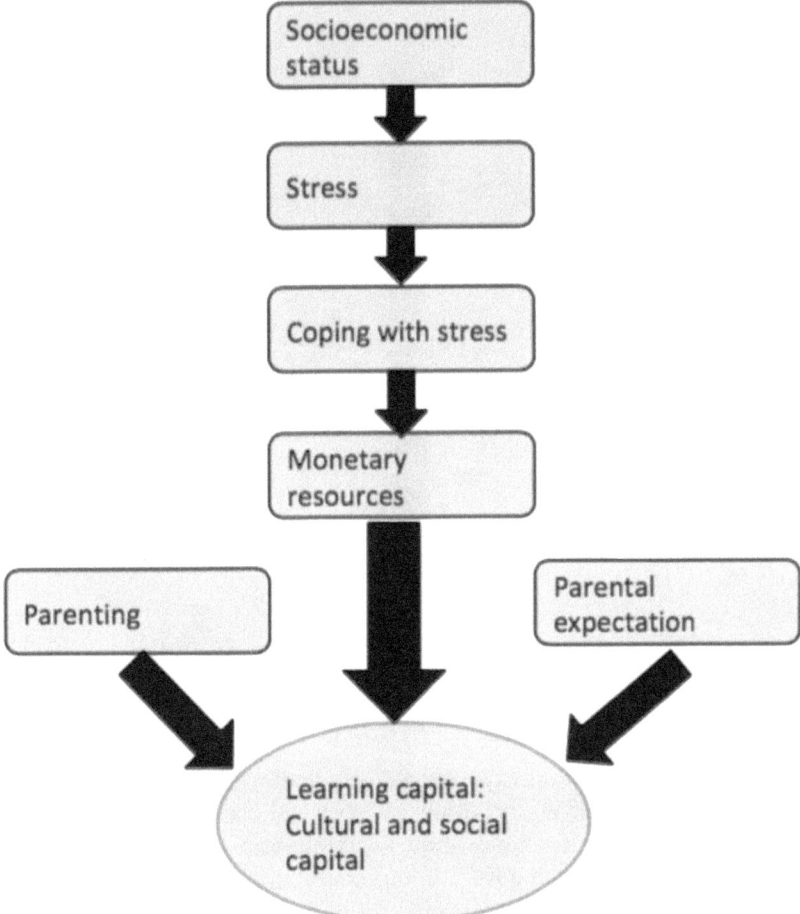

Figure 2.2 Stage 1: Prerequisite of Tracking Students into Low Caliber Class. *Source*: Lam, 2014, p. 327.

Lam notes that people may develop reactive-responding toward a depressed event—including chronic vigilance, acting on the basis of environmental demands rather than self-generated goals, having simple short-term goals, developing a narrow range of skills, maintaining a present orientation, reacting emotionally, and using few options to deal with environmental demands. Impoverished parents are often depressed, have learned helplessness, have low-esteem, and lack goals and motivation to cope with poverty. Additionally, parents tend to have low expectations of children, but also the children do of themselves as well do their teachers.

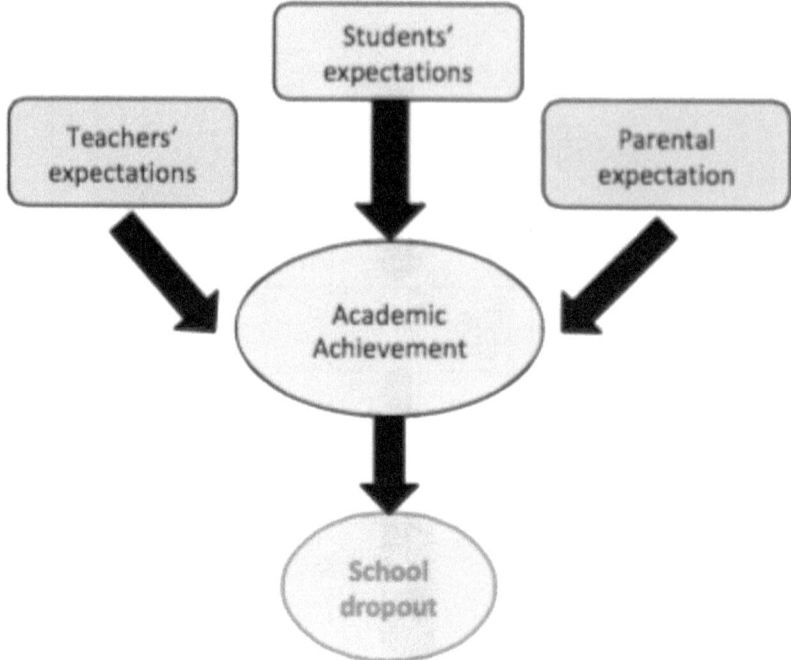

Figure 2.3 Stage 2: A Triad Nexus of Expectation. *Source*: Lam, 2014, p. 327.

The nexus of the triad of expectations (see figure 2.3) among parents, children, and teachers intertwines with each other and bears a large influence on children's academic performance. Low expectations placed on children can be exhibited from their learning motivation. Learning motivation is defined as a "student's tendency to find academic activities meaningful and worthwhile and to try to derive the intended academic benefits from them" (Lam, 2014, p. 329).

As Lam elucidates, learning motivation is a dichotomy of mastery goals and performance goals; the dichotomy differs in terms of the nature, strategies, controllability, and locus of control (p. 329). People who set mastery goals are ones who strive for personal growth. To acquire knowledge, people make attempts, including mistakes, and they perceive having a high internal locus of control by attributing both success and failure to internal factors such as effort (Lam, 2014).

In contrast, students who adopt the performance approach employ the effective learning strategy to aim for success; the effective learning strategy is to target the easiest task and to abandon the most difficult task as it will probably end in failure. Both views—performance approach and performance avoidance—attribute events to an external locus of control; people who are performance avoidant have the tendency to avoid failure. Failures trigger a negative feeling so students do not exert effort for improvement (Lam, 2014).

If we go back to the dichotomy of learning motivation and academic performance, it seems that learning motivation is vital to positive academic performance; however, a question remains unanswered: how does learning motivation mediate the relationship between socioeconomic status and academic performance? Students from poor families exhibit performance avoidance in a way that they have a low expectation for success and attribute this thought process to an external locus of control (Lam, 2014).

Prior to interacting with low socioeconomic students, teachers already form expectations toward students. This expectation is associated with students with low ability in terms of school attendance, attitudes, learning, motivation, and academic outcomes (Lam, 2014). Teachers have negative stereotypes because of tracking—the culprit to assign students from poor families to classes with low ability: "Teachers have been found to devote less positive attention to students from low socioeconomic backgrounds and to praise their positive performance less" (p. 330).

In Alfie Kohn's article "Poor Teaching for Poor Children . . . in the Name of Reform," he wrote:

> The problem isn't that education lacks "rigor"—in fact, a single-minded focus on "raising the bar" has served mostly to push more low-income youths out of school—but that it lacks depth and relevance and the capacity to engage students. (p. np)

Crandall and Kurtz (2011) add:

> Rather than engaging with education as a banking system in which we deposit nuggets of information into our students' heads for them to withdraw during the test, we see education as a house we can build together, and each house, with a different team of co-builders, is going to look a little bit different. (p. 57)

Rapidly increasing impoverishment among children has lasting negative consequences on the educational attainment and economic success of the next generation (Guo, 1998). Under extreme environmental conditions, whatever genetic potential for language, height, or intellectual functioning a child has, that potential is unable to be expressed. The powerful and awful environment in which such children live suppress the expression of whatever genes that child has for complete mastery of language, for full height, for complete intellectual functioning, and for competency in social relationships (Berliner, 2006).

This is the same point made by evolutionary biologist Richard Lewontin, who discussed how two genetically identical seeds of corns planted in very different plots of earth would grow to very different heights. In the plot with good soil, sufficient water, and sunshine, genetics accounts for almost all of the noticeable variation in the plants, while environment is much less of a factor in the variation that we see (Berliner, 2006).

On the other hand, when the soil, water, and sun are not appropriate, genetics do not account for much of the noticeable variation among the lower-growing and often sickly plants that are our harvest; genes do not have a chance to express themselves under poor environmental conditions. There is strong evidence that the influence of genes on intelligence is quite dependent on social class (Berliner, 2006, p. 969).

Ability is a more stable individual trait than achievement and tends to be determined by both environmental and genetic factors early in life. Achievement on the other hand is more acquired. It is not only a function of ability, but also of motivation and opportunities; long-term poverty has substantial influences on both ability and achievement (Guo, 1998, p. 260). The socioeconomic influences of young children may be very different from those on older children because these influences may interact with a child's biological and cognitive development. Much that shapes the final human product takes place in the home during the first years of life.

There exists a critical period in a child's life when the child must be exposed to certain experiences, or lasting damage will be done to his or her cognitive development. Later cognitive development may be, to a large extent, contingent on the cognitive response systems acquired early in life. The critical period includes the beginning of elementary school when children are acquiring basic skills and academic self-images.

While ability is more a measure of the rate of learning, achievement is more a measure of what is learned. Compared with achievement, ability is a more stable individual trait. Compared with ability, achievement is more similar to learned skills. In that sense, achievement is more public, and therefore, more a product of environment and social interactions (Guo, 1998). According to Guo, that ability, in that sense, is more private and individual, and therefore less a product of contextual effects. Achievement is very much a function of ability, but not ability alone: "Whether individuals realize, fail to realize, or exceed their intellectual potential is often heavily influenced by factors such as motivation and opportunity" (Guo, 1998, p. 264).

As a relatively stable human trait and substantially determined by genetic factors, ability is probably developed early in life. If poverty is to have a negative impact on ability, the impact should be the most visible while ability is being developed in early life. Scholars define ability as "developed ability or rate of learning." Developed ability depends very much on innate ability, but the formation of developed ability also depends on environment.

Cumulative family poverty exerts important influences on children's cognitive development. Poverty experienced during early adolescence after childhood is particularly important for achievement. Poverty experienced in early adolescence as opposed to childhood is more influential on achievement because achievement is very much a function of motivation and opportunity and because an impoverished environment is more likely to affect a child's motivation and opportunity when the child becomes an adolescent (Guo, 1998).

Guo explains that childhood appears to be a much more crucial period for development of cognitive ability than early adolescence. Poverty cumulated over childhood has a more detrimental effect on childhood ability than poverty cumulated from about birth to early adolescence, or poverty experienced in early adolescence has on early adolescent ability. It is likely that childhood ability is more malleable than early adolescence ability. This argument explains why poverty has a much larger effect on ability measured in childhood than ability measured in early adolescence (Guo, 1998).

Ability, as a more permanent trait than achievement, once formed, may be less susceptible to disadvantaged environments. The stronger effects of poverty are on older children's achievement. When the habits, skills, or cognitive structures that are preconditions for new learning have not been obtained, new learning will be impaired. Because subsequent learning depends upon prior learning, learning deficits are cumulative.

Early exposure to poverty is linked to children's future functioning along multiple domains, including behavior problems, self-regulatory skills, and academic performance (Roy & Raver, 2014). A clear, detrimental relationship exists between growing up in a poor family and children's cognitive functioning and academic performance. Poverty is a predictive compromise in children's executive function and self-regulatory skills (Roy & Raver, 2014). Families facing poverty are also more likely to experience other life stressors (e.g., loss of a job, inability to pay bills) that may exacerbate the strains of poverty and negatively affect their children's cognitive skills and behavior problems.

Economically disadvantaged children receive less cognitive stimulation: they are read to less often, watch more television, and often attend lower quality daycare. Children who grow up in poverty arrive in kindergarten less well prepared to learn, placing them at long-term academic risk. Disadvantaged children also underperform across multiple indicators of cognitive functioning. These include assessments of general intelligence, speed of cognitive processing, language ability, and executive function (Fitzpatrick et al., 2014).

It is possible that individual differences in executive functions partially account for economically based differences in child school readiness: "Executive functions are believed to emerge as a function of the development of neural networks in the prefrontal cortex" (Fitzpatrick et al., 2014, p. 25). As children reach school age, executive function skills can help children hold information or instructions in mind during classroom activities, focus on task-relevant stimuli during problem-solving tasks, and resist internal or external distractions.

From kindergarten to high school, executive functions have been shown to explain an important proportion of the variance in achievement, even after accounting for the child's IQ and SES (Fitzpatrick et al., 2014). Executive function skills are likely to contribute to achievement because they support the mechanisms of learning and help children remain focused on task-relevant information in the midst of distractions. As a result, executive function skills can facilitate children's performance and learning in the classroom setting.

Furthermore, early vocabulary knowledge also explains part of socio-economically based disparities in early achievement, as well as part of the association between executive functions and achievement. Strong verbal skills are likely to support both executive functioning and classroom learning (Fitzpatrick et al., 2014). For example, better verbal skills can help children use internalized speech to give themselves directions during problem-solving activities.

The environments of children growing up in poverty tend to be characterized by more stress as well as the absence of key experiences that help foster strong executive function skills. The families of disadvantaged children tend to provide less warmth, stability, and support. Research has shown that the experience of stressful environments early in life can also alter children's physiological stress reactivity. A less adaptive pattern of stress reactivity is then associated with poor executive function development. Children who grow up in poverty are likely to display more externalizing behavior and be less task-oriented and engaged in learning (Fitzpatrick et al., 2014).

Enhancing the executive function skills of disadvantaged children may help reduce socioeconomically based disparities in school readiness. Inexpensive, easy to implement programs can effectively enhance executive function skills in young children before they begin formal schooling. In addition, because vocabulary skills appear to play an important role in school readiness, improving the literacy environment of economically disadvantaged households is also likely to help children arrive at school better prepared to meet the challenges of the classroom. The progress of a society depends on the education of its population; enhancing executive functioning and literacy skills in preschool-aged children may increase the chances that all children are equipped to learn on the first day of school (Fitzpatrick et al., 2014).

The development of productive capacities in the form of cognitive skills is a key mechanism through which education acquires economic value, both to individuals and society; and the imperative to upskill the labor force is central to the economic rationale for educational expansion and improvement (Rolleston, 2014). The age at which a child initially enrolls in school is an important influence on the total exposure to schooling likely to be received. Later enrolling children are typically more disadvantaged and may also, as a result, experience pressure to leave school earlier than more advantaged pupils, especially where later states of education are associated with rising costs (Rolleston, 2014).

REFERENCES

BBC News. (2015, October 14). PISA test tops 40 for maths and reading. http://www.bbc.com/news/business-26249042.

Berliner, D. C. (2006). Our impoverished view of educational research. *Teachers College Record, 108*(6), 949–995.

Crandall, J., & Kutz, S. (2011). Ranking and sorting and labeling: Driving aboriginal students out of schools. *Our Schools/Our Selves, 21*(1), 57–65.

Edwards, S. (2012). The effects of poverty on achievement gap: A quantitative analysis using stratification theory. *Proceedings of the National Conference on Undergraduate Research (NCUR)*, 1351–1358. http://www.ncurproceedings.org/ojs/index.php/NCUR2012/article/view/641.

Fitzpatrick, C., McKinnon, R. D., Blair, C. B., & Willoughby, M. T. (2014). Do preschool executive function skills explain the school readiness gap between advantaged and disadvantaged children? *Learning and Instruction, 30*, 25–31. doi:10.1016/j.learninstruc.2013.11.003.

Guo, G. (1998). The timing of the influences of cumulative poverty on children's cognitive ability and achievement. *Social Forces, 77*(1), 257–288.

Jerrim, J., & Vignoles, A. (2013). Social mobility, regression to the mean and the cognitive development of high ability children from disadvantaged homes. *Journal of the Royal Statistical Society, 176*(4), 887–906.

Kohn, A. (2011, April 27). Poor teaching for poor children . . . in the name of reform. *Education Week*, p. np.

Lam, G. (2014). A theoretical framework of the relation between socioeconomic status and academic achievement of students. *Education, 134*(3), 326–331.

Marston, D. C. (2013). Neurobehavioral effects of poverty. American Psychological Association: The SES Indicator.

Mulvey, J., & Cooper, B. S. (2012). *Intersections of children's health, education and welfare*. New York: Palgrave Macmillan.

Rolleston, C. (2014). Learning profiles and the "skills gap" in four developing countries: A comparative analysis of schooling and skills development. *Oxford Review of Education, 40*(1), 132–150. doi:10.1080/03054985.2013.873528.

Roy, A. L., & Raver, C. C. (2014). Are all risks equal? Early experiences of poverty-related risk and children's functioning. *Journal of Family Psychology, 28*(3), 391–400. doi:10.1037/a0036683.

Chapter 3

How Early Is Early Enough?

Janet D. Mulvey

Language acquisition, understanding, and application are the first prerequisites for learning. We know the differences in readiness for children who reside in different socioeconomic circumstances. On average, the difference in language between the poor and the more affluent is vast. By the time children reach third grade, according to Klein and Knitzer (2007) for the National Center for Children in Poverty, those who live in middle-class educated families have a vocabulary of approximately 12,000 words versus 4,000 words for children in poverty.

Failure to recognize the reasons behind success and failure has placed the United States at the 50th percentile in educational attainment as compared to other worldwide industrialized nations. Instituting a universal preschool program (as Mayor Bill de Blasio did in New York City) is a good start, but school readiness language must be internalized before the age of three.

The difference in language acquisition and vocabulary development is just one of the many reasons of school failure among those who live in environments of poverty. Physical, emotional, and cognitive developments are affected within the family, neighborhood, and community. Combating the educational effects of poverty requires a state and nationwide commitment to eradicating the loss of potential human capital for positive gain.

Early child care has an effect on the cognitive development and readiness to enter the formal education setting. Children born into poverty often suffer consequences physically, emotionally, and cognitively. At the educational level, they enter school with fewer skills that become exacerbated as more demands for learning emerge.

Environmental factors experienced from birth through early childhood have physical effects on the brain. The official measures of poverty rates, in the United States, increased from 12.5 percent in 2007 to 21.8 percent in 2012 (Stanford Center Poverty Report, 2014). Too many children born and raised in these poverty environments suffer the consequences of poor nutrition, polluted neighborhoods, familial stressed conditions, and poor quality education.

A 2013 study conducted by the Washington University School of Medicine (Luby et al., 2013) found that impoverished conditions affect the development of the white and gray matters of the brain. Each is important in the cognitive development of the child: the gray matter serves to process information to other areas of the brain. It is a communication system that connects sensory systems including the central nervous system. The white matter on the other hand has often been referred to as the "subway for the brain" (Balm, 2014). The white matter is a railway system that connects different regions of the brain and communicates information from one area to the next.

The image of the brain in figure 3.1 provides a visual representation of the brain's lobes and their relationship to learning.

The cerebrum is the largest part of the brain associated with higher function in thought and action. Four sections, as illustrated in the visual, represent the cerebral cortex. Labeled "lobes" they are the frontal, parietal, occipital, and temporal lobes. The development of each is critical to the process of learning in the early and later years.

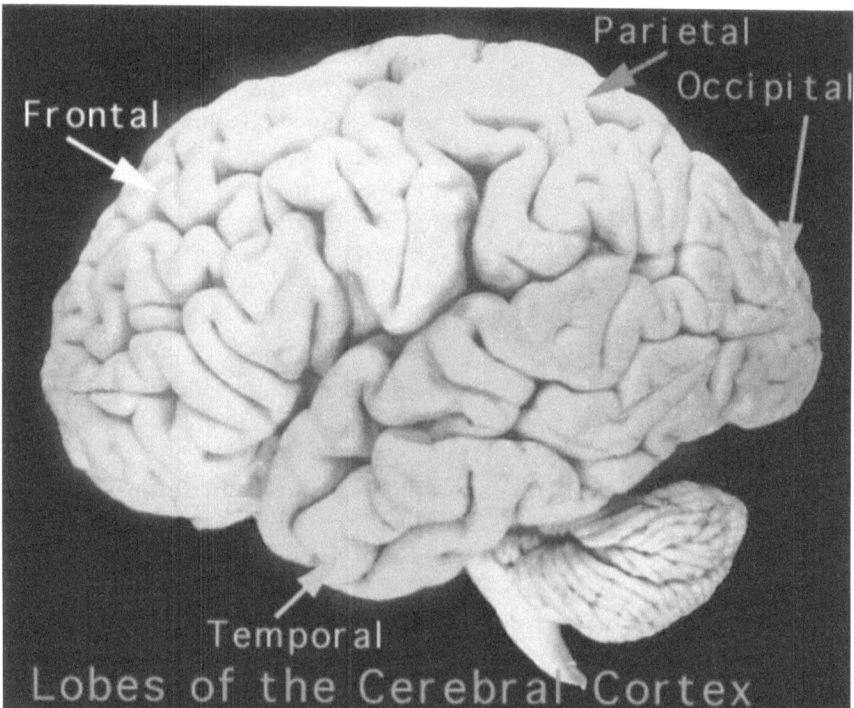

Figure 3.1 Adapted from an image at coachhouserehab.com/images/brain.jpg.

Learning is dependent upon

1. The ability to problem solve, planning, parts of speech, reasoning, and emotional pragmatism are all associated with the frontal lobe of the brain.
2. The understanding and implementation of movement, orientation, recognition, and discrimination of stimuli are associated with the parietal lobe.
3. Visual processing is essential and associated with the occipital lobe.
4. The ability to perceive and recognize auditory stimuli, recall (or memory), and speech is associated with the temporal lobe. (Source: https://www.google.com/search?q=images+of+parietal+and+frontal+regions+of+the+brain&espv=)

The brain is the body's computer, with connections that need stability to process all the necessary information, skill development, and reasoning necessary for educational and societal success. Jensen (2009) stresses that

> socioeconomic status forms a huge part of this equation. Children raised in poverty rarely choose to behave differently, but they are faced daily with overwhelming challenges that affluent children never have to confront, and their brains have adapted to suboptimal conditions in ways that undermine good school performance. (p. 21)

School-age children brought up in impoverished conditions perform lower on cognitive ability tests than their more affluent peers. Teachers report that not only are the children lacking in prerequisite language skills but often have difficulty in attending to lessons. The frustration in lack of success results in behavioral difficulties contributing to academic failure.

Policy makers and politicians must stop blaming families, schools, and teachers, and become educated themselves in the causes and prevention of school failure. Leadership within the local, state, and national governments must themselves become educated to begin the process of change to better schools and environments. Then and only then will we see policies that support the improvements for a child's right to opportunity for an education and a better, healthier life.

ENVIRONMENT, NUTRITION, AND HEALTH CARE

Without proper nutrition, even the infant in utero may be at risk for poor mental and physical health. According to Ziol-Guest (as cited in Kelley, 2012), "That being poor when you are in utero doubles your risk for early onset of . . . diseases is shocking." This affects children's ability to earn a better salary in their employable years.

This chapter examines the early readiness principles that must be in place before a child enters into formal schooling. We report on the research associated with developmental milestones in language and social/emotional readiness. Policy and political failure to pass the funding that invests in our children and families perpetuates and stagnates mobility opportunities and weakens potential human capital.

The implications for learning and success in today's standards are great. Less language skill in reading, writing, and speaking can lead to less readiness, a likely failure on standardized tests, and greater frustration, depreciating engagement, and ultimately to the probability of dropping out of school. A look at statistics for children's readiness from an early age and their success/failure throughout their educational lives shows the importance of understanding implications from prebirth on.

FROM BIRTH TO FIVE YEARS OF AGE

Children born to mothers who have lived in poverty often have not had the prenatal care afforded by the middle and higher socioeconomic groups. And while this has decreased over the years for minority Black, Hispanic, and Asian Pacific groups, the trend for lack of prenatal care among teenage mothers has remained high.

The graph in figure 3.2 accessed from Child Trends (2013) displays the percentage of teenage births related to lack of prenatal care. The implications for children born under these circumstances usually place them at a distinct disadvantage for educational success and economic stability. In a statistical study done by Planned Parenthood, in 2011 an estimated 9 percent of births were by teens younger than nineteen years of age.

Parenting skills among the young and poor are also factors for continued school failure and social mobility. Hoffman (2008) and Breheny and Stephens (2007) cite the following about teenage mothers:

- They have lower family incomes.
- They are more likely to be poor and receive public assistance.
- They are less educated.
- Their children lag in standards of early development.

The significance of the data relates to the intergenerational tendency for the daughters of teen mothers to, themselves, give birth during their own teen years. In a study done by Meade, Kershaw, and Ickovics (2008), risk factors were examined through an ecological approach. The result of the study found that "66% of daughters born to teenage mothers were more likely to become teenage mothers" (2008, p. 27). The study included performance in school, environmental factors, ethnicity, and poverty.

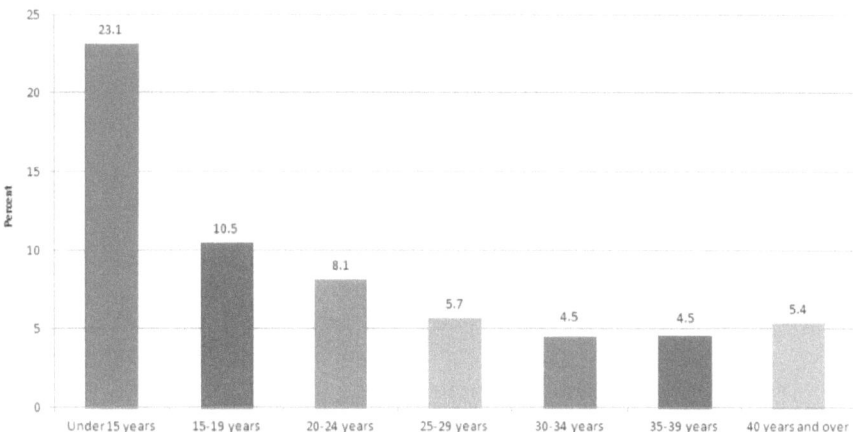

Figure 3.2 Retrieved from Child Trends Data Bank (2013). Late or no prenatal care. www.childtrends.org/indicators=late-or-no-prenatal-care. *Note:* Data exclude those jurisdictions using the 1989 revision of the birth certificate (ten states, representing 13 percent of births). *Source*: United States Department of Health and Human Services (US DHHS), Centers for Disease Control and Prevention (CDC), National Center for Health Statistics (NCHS), Division of Vital Statistics, Natality public-use data 2007–2013, on CDC WONDER online database. Available at wonder.cdc.gov/natality-current.html.

Studies have found that children born to teen mothers often lack the necessary communication skills needed for school readiness. They have not been exposed to books or read to by their teen mothers; vocabulary is limited and general support for school activities is lacking. This lack of readiness perpetuates difficulties in school causing failure, dropping out, and living on public assistance following a disturbing pattern without resolve unless policy makers and politicians see the value of breaking the cycle.

Studies further indicate the comparative rate of readiness for academic success between children born to young mothers who have not completed their own education and those older with high school completion. Cognitive and academic readiness is greatly reduced for children born into an impoverished environment and to mothers who are seventeen years and younger. According to Hofferth and Reid (2003), children born to mothers unprepared for parenthood have their childhood development effected. "In comparison with the children of women who became mothers as adults, the children of teenage mothers score lower on achievement tests and higher on behavioral problems" (p. 46).

The political battle over Planned Parenthood, based upon religious rather than scientific studies, misses the point on unwanted and unplanned pregnancies. Prevention rather than intervention allows the teen to mature, finish school, and eliminates many of the issues for the unwanted, unexpected, and unprepared for child.

While the children of teen mothers too often suffer the consequences of their environments, all children born into an impoverished state are more than likely to struggle in school, and in life. We are aware of conditions such as asthma and others caused by poor nutrition and polluted environments. A new Cornell study, led by researcher Kathleen Ziol-Guest looks into the early onset of diseases, affecting children we often associate with an older generation. Goldblum (2012) reports that the study found that "living in poverty—even in utero—can lead to a lifetime of poor health" (p. np).

The study tracked people who were born into poverty, examining the conditions in which they were born into through two years of age. As adults they suffered from arthritis, hypertension, and poor health by the age of thirty.

Asthma is a leading chronic disease that is suffered by children and adolescents in the United States. The loss of time in school exacerbates learning failure especially for poor and minority children. The Center for Disease Control and Prevention (2015) report, "Low-income populations, minorities, and children living in inner cities experience more emergency department visits, hospitalizations, and deaths due to asthma than the general population" (p. np).

Asthma attacks for these children are often caused by both indoor and outdoor environmental factors. Buildings in crowded poverty areas contain lead, dust mites, tobacco smoke, and other irritants labeled asthma triggers where the children are constantly exposed.

The absenteeism for these youngsters, as well as the daily struggle and stress of feeling ill, affects their ability to attend and learn. The lack of adequate clinical preventative measures exacerbates the condition, resulting in long-term absenteeism or, in too many cases, death. And even when in school, attending to lessons and learning are almost impossible when hunger or malaise interferes.

Compare the performance of children who have experienced good prenatal care, adequate nutrition, positive parenting, and safe and clean environments with those who experience little or no prenatal care, inadequate nutrition, stressful home and polluted environments. How is it that local, state, and national policy makers have little or no knowledge of basic biology influencing physical, emotional, or cognitive growth?

Pollution and Development

In a study conducted at the UCLA Institute of the Environment and Sustainability (Ritz & Wilhelm, 2008), a report was issued on a thirteen-year study measuring the effects of pollution on babies born into highly affected areas. The results are undeniable: areas with high levels of toxins can cause adverse effects on the unborn fetus, low birth weight, physical and neurological developmental delays, heart defects, and asthma. Resulting medical conditions affect attendance in school, illnesses that inhibit attention to learning, and a life sentence of low or impoverished living conditions.

The time between conception and birth is perhaps one of the most vulnerable life stages, during which the environment may have tremendous immediate and lasting effects on health. The fetus undergoes rapid growth and organ development and the maternal environment helps direct these processes, for better or for worse.

Evidence is accumulating that environmental exposures can cause infants to be born premature (before 37 weeks of gestation) or low weight (less than 2500 grams, or 5.5 pounds), or to be born with certain birth defects. These babies are far more likely to die in infancy, and those who survive have high risks of brain, respiratory, and digestive problems in early life. The impact of environmental exposures on fetal development may be far reaching, as data suggest growth and developmental delays in utero influence the risk for heart disease and diabetes in adulthood.

Perhaps the most recent reports on highly polluted areas show that the only constant is poverty, ignoring geographical differences in urban and/or suburban regions. We associate pollution with high population density in such cities as New York, Detroit, or Los Angeles, but dumping and hazardous waste sites are more prevalent in areas where the poor reside.

For example, low-income people, mostly of color, live in a ring of toxins in Richmond, California. According to Kay and Katz (2012), numerous studies by health and governmental agencies document that those who live near highly congested highways and seaports contract severe health problems and die much earlier than their more affluent opposites. Kay and Katz go on to report, "Children have a greater risk of impaired lung function and babies are more likely to be born prematurely" (p. np). It has been documented that those who are exposed to diesel exhaust and other contaminants have a higher risk of cancer, heart attacks, and strokes.

The constant exposure to contaminants during childhood lowers cognitive functioning, resulting in poorer opportunity for success in school and less chance for employment to move them from the polluted neighborhoods in which they are doomed.

Connections between cognition and urban pollution have been scientifically studied and established in cities across the nation. Suglia et al. (2008) found that while genetic factors play a role, the Particulate Matter (black carbon) "predicted decreased cognitive function across assessments of verbal and nonverbal intelligence and memory constructs" (pp. 281–282).

How is it we compare standard scores on state-driven tests without knowledge of why the discrepancies are so great between the lower and more affluent school districts? Why have we relegated more choice with less support for our public school system?

The education policies set by the government, in an attempt to improve our standing, internationally, miss the mark on all points. Comparing our education system with the highest performing countries without comparing the funding, equality of opportunity, health care, and school support is acting in ignorance. According to a report by the OECD:

> Socio-economic disadvantage has a notable impact on student performance in the United States: 15% of the variation in student performance in the United States is explained by students' socio-economic status, similar to the OECD average, but with some improvement since 2003. This contrasts with less than 10% in a number of countries/economies, including Finland, Hong Kong-China, Japan and Norway. In other words, in the United States, two students from a different socio-economic background vary much more in their learning outcomes than is normally the case in these other countries/economies. (OECD, 2012, p. 4)

Instituting national mandated testing and comparing schools within different economic areas can only be accurate if all services that enhance cognitive potential are met. Norway is a perfect example. While there are economic differences among the population, all children have access to national health care, preschools ("kindergartens") that are mandates and all resources and teacher salaries are standardized. Thus, the system is designed to assure that the next generation will be able to sustain the country's growth and economic prosperity.

Governance with Knowledge

Policy makers need to become educated on the cost to the nation of those who do not complete at least a high school education. There is a lack of understanding or acceptance that poverty is the road to failure that can be fixed and improve the quality of life for all children, adults, and the nation. According to Angel Gurría (2010): "Success will go to those individuals and countries which are swift to adapt, slow to complain and open to change" (p. 5).

According to Barber and Mourshed (2007), the top eleven performing educational programs internationally are, in alphabetical order:

- Alberta, Canada
- Australia
- Belgium
- Finland
- Hong Kong
- Japan
- Netherlands

- New Zealand
- Ontario
- Singapore
- South Korea

What is it that these programs offer to advance them for recognition? How do they differ from the norm?

Cultural differences, educational standard demands, and diverse governances seem to remove the notion or reasons of specific areas affecting successful performance. Teacher quality, differentiated instruction, targeted support where needed, and adequate funding are the constancies that tie these successful school programs together (Barber & Mourshed, 2007).

The 2012 PISA report indicates a continuing trend in underperforming, especially in mathematics. While the United States is close to average in literacy, the comparison places the country on a level with the less developed countries in the world in math. Table 3.1 shows the average score internationally, the ranking of the United States in relation to the mean score, percentage of students above and below the mean, and the annualized growth:

Table 3.1

	PISA Mean Score	United States	Percent Above	Percent Below	Percent Annualized growth
Mathematics	494	481	8.8	25.8	−1.4
Reading	496	498			
Science	501	497			+1.4

Thirty-four countries are ranked on the PISA: the United States ranks twenty-sixth in math, seventeenth in reading, and twenty-first in science. Why the difference? What needs to be done? How can we change policy to effect positive change for all students?

Rivers and Sanders reported on results from a research-based data-driven project on teacher quality in Tennessee. The findings after a ten-year study revealed a 50 percent difference in performance between students who had higher quality teachers over a three-year period.

Scientific Facts and Governmental Policies

The studies are in and they are clear: poverty in America has remained and offers an almost constant lack of opportunity, unhealthy living, and hopelessness. Beginning life in an impoverished environment is too often a life sentence. Unhealthy childhood, poor education, and lack of opportunity result in minimum wage jobs supplemented with government assistance and sometimes criminal activity. Statistically more poor Black men are incarcerated, costing the nation more per year than supporting public schools and education. According to a report by DeFina and Hannon (2013), more than 60 percent of those incarcerated are African American or Hispanic with earned incomes under $12,000 annually. Where do we begin?

In an empirical study done in many geographical regions in the United States and the United Kingdom (see Burger, 2010), early childhood education beginning at age three has produced positive results. According to the study, "Favorable effects of model interventions diminish social inequalities due to differences in socio-economic status" (p. 160). Learning prerequisite skills prior to entering kindergarten levels the playing field for success in school and hopefully in life.

Early education, intervention, and parental instruction must be a step taken to ready children for formal schooling. It is imperative to equalize skills, language, health, and social communication for students near and below the poverty line.

Schools themselves need to be welcoming, sanitary, safe, attractive, and free of pollutants that aggravate and induce asthmatic occurrences. Attracting educators for high quality instruction, making the profession a desirable vocation, assuring the right type of training, and implementing instructional practices to meet the needs of the individual child must be goals if we are to advance our standing internationally.

Teachers must be specifically trained to understand, communicate, and be an integral part of the community in and outside of the neighborhoods in which they teach. The importance of training and supporting preschool education should be a priority. Professionals working with three- to five-year-olds need specific education on cognitive processes, brain development, stages of language acquisition, and its relationship to all academic areas. We must not negate the importance of scientific evidence for early childhood development. Shonkoff and Phillips (2000) in their book *From Neurons to Neighborhoods* provide compelling evidence for early childhood development, "All children are wired for feelings and ready to learn . . . early environments matter . . . and the course of development can be altered in early childhood by effective interventions" (p. 23).

Early childhood teachers are too often the least educated with fewer requirements than the elementary through high school teachers. And yet the first five years of a child's life are the most important with either promise or vulnerability for future success.

Perhaps a large component of helping with early childcare is educating the parents who bear them. As reported earlier, teen mothers' babies often have low weight and have not had the opportunity for prenatal care. These children are the most vulnerable for long-term health and learning problems.

Evidence of success with very early (infant) childcare/education and their young mothers was clearly shown back in 1972 when the Abecedarian Project was conducted. A carefully and controlled scientific longitudinal study examined the effects of intervention for infants born into impoverished conditions over a five-year period. To compare the effects of intervention, 111 children were placed into either a control group where there was no intervention compared to the experimental group where intensive intervention was conducted and where the mothers were trained to continue the practices at home.

Children in the experimental groups received educational intervention from infancy through age five. All children were followed and their growth assessed at ages twelve, fifteen, twenty-one, thirty, and thirty-five. The results were consistent with overall better performance through elementary and high school. More of the experimental group attended four-year colleges, received bachelor's degrees, and hold better paying jobs.

Interestingly, a new 2014 study on the benefits of early childhood care and intervention follows suit. Scientists from the University College of London and University of Chicago and spearheaded by James Heckman, Nobel Prize winner, did an "intricate statistical analysis" and found "that people who had received high-quality early care and education in the 1970s through the project are healthier now—significant measures also indicate better health lies ahead for them" (Heckman, 2014).

EARLY PRESCHOOL THROUGH THE ELEMENTARY YEARS

Early childhood programs connected to community schools are essential, especially for those who do not have the opportunity for enrichment during their young developing years. Qualified early childhood specialists who understand the physical, emotional, and cognitive development of children from infancy to age five can make a lifelong difference for children who live in underprivileged communities.

Upon reaching primary school age, health and nutrition clinics should be part of the school environment for easy access to health care and education on healthier, more nutritious meals. Understanding the community demographic and needs sets the tone for establishment of healthy friendly schools that help mitigate the environment outside.

Even in poorer communities, high quality teachers make the difference. Trained in developmental stages of learning and understanding particular needs of children in a community increases the learning, success, and motivation to continue learning throughout their school years. Principal leaders in less affluent schools should have the expertise in communicating with the community, setting a climate of welcome and assistance. Partnering with outside agencies, services from health care, counseling, and adult education, can create a more positive and supportive school environment for the children. According to Barber and Mourshed (2007), "In all of the systems we studied, the ability of a school system to attract the right people into teaching is closely linked to the status of the profession" (p. 30).

Bilingual Education

The United States like many countries around the globe has seen an increase in immigrant migration seeking safety or an opportunity for a better life. Influx of immigrants from all countries has placed an enormous responsibility on the education community. Children from families where English has never been spoken often suffer the frustration of learning and succeeding in school. Controversy continues on the best way to help children assimilate and prosper into the American culture: bilingual classes or complete immersion into English-only classrooms?

According to a study by the Pew Research Center (2015), the number of immigrants, younger than seventeen will outnumber non-Hispanic whites by 2050. At present, one out of four children is an immigrant or a child born to a recent immigrant and schools are struggling to meet their needs. The demand for standardized testing negates the opportunity to provide time for assimilation, bicultural integration, and multiple vocabulary strategies for effective bilingual efficiency.

SUMMARY

The United States continues to fall behind in its effort to teach our children well. The huge chasm separating the economically wealthy and poor schools threatens to keep us behind the other industrialized countries in the world. Political agendas should not influence the classroom. Each village, town, city, and state has diverse populations and economic needs. A national standard set forth by the government guarantees inequity and curricula programs that cannot meet the needs of all, especially those in impoverished areas or newly immigrated.

Scientific research reinforces the need for healthy beginnings in life. Cognitive development begins in utero and continues throughout the early childhood years. For children born into low-income areas without adequate health care and/or parental sophistication, success in school becomes a struggle. Failure to meet education standards results in grade retention, failure to complete, low-income jobs, and perpetuation into the next generation.

Early childhood programs that use assessment to determine the learning paths necessary for success should be individualized and focused upon the needs of that child. Cognitive growth can be stimulated with the right environment and tools. Childhood experiences prior to the age of four can stimulate the areas of the brain "dedicated to language and cognition" (Farah, 2012).

Farah goes on to state, "The development of the cortex in the late teens was closely associated with the child's cognitive stimulation at the age of 4" (p. np). All evidence from scientific research on brain development, school success, and mobility opportunity point to early childhood education. Spending money for children who would otherwise miss this early life experience can create a healthier, better educated, and more productive individual for society.

Politicians, policy makers, and educational leaders must listen to the evidence and act on behalf of the children to benefit all.

REFERENCES

Balm, J. (2014). The subway of the brain—why white matter matters. *BioMed Central.* http://www.iapsych.com/im/brainsubway.pdf.

Barber, M., & Mourshed, M. (2007). *How the world's best-performing school systems come out on top.* London: McKinsey and Company.

Burger, K. (2010). How does early childhood care and education affect cognitive development? An international review of the effects of early interventions for children from different social backgrounds. *Early Childhood Research Quarterly,* 25(2), 140–165.

Breheny, M., & Stephens, C. (2007). Individual responsibility and social restraint: The construction of adolescent motherhood in social scientific research. *Culture, Health, & Sexuality,* 9(4), 333–46.

Center for Disease Control and Prevention. (2015, June 17). Asthma and schools. https://www.cdc.gov/healthyschools/asthma/index.htm.

Child Trends Data Bank. (2013). Late or no prenatal care. www.childtrends.org/indicators=late-or-no-prenatal-care.

DeFina, R., & Hannon, L. (2013). The impact of mass incarceration on poverty. *Crime and Delinquency,* (59), 562–586.

Farah, M. (2012, October 17). *Childhood stimulation key to brain development, study finds.* Presented at the annual meeting of the Society for Neuroscience.

Goldblum, J. (2012). Poor babies set up for a lifetime of illness. *Huffington Post.* www.huffingtonpost.com/joanne-goldblum/child-poverty_b_2218208.html.

Gurría, A. (2010). Foreword. In OECD (2010), *PISA 2009 results: What makes a school successful?-Resources, policies and practices* (volume IV). http://dx.doi.org/10.1787/9789264091559-en.

Heckman, J. (2014). *The economics of human potential.* heckmanequation.org.
Hofferth, S. L., & Reid, L. (2003). Early childbearing and children's achievement and behavior over time. *Perspectives on Sexual and Reproductive Health, 34*(1), 41–49.
Hoffman, S. D. (2006). By the numbers. *The Public Cost of Teen Child-Bearing.* Washington, DC: National Campaign to Prevent Teen and Unplanned Pregnancy.
Jensen, E. (2009). *Teaching with poverty in mind.* Alexandria, VA: ASCD Publications.
Kay, J., & Katz, C. (2012, June 4). Pollution, poverty, people of color: The factory on the hill. *Environmental Health News.* http://www.environmentalhealthnews.org/ehs/news/2012/pollution-poverty-and-people-of-color-richmond-day-1.
Kelley, S. (2012). Poor kids twice as likely to suffer from arthritis, hypertension in adulthood. *Cornell Chronicle.* http://www.news.cornell.edu/stories/2012.
Klein, L. G. & Kitzer, J. (2007). Promoting effective early learning. National Center for Children in Poverty.
Luby, J., et al. (2013). The effects of poverty on childhood brain development: The mediating effect of caregiving and stressful life effects. *JAMA Pediatrics, 167*(2), 1135–1142.
Meade, C. S., Kershaw, T. S., & Ickovics, J. R. (2008). The intergenerational cycle of teenage motherhood: An ecological approach. *Health Psychology,* (4), 419–429. doi: 10.103/0278-6133,27.4.419.
Munoz, C. (2010). On how age affects foreign language learning. *Advances in Research on Language Acquisition and Teaching.* Selected Papers, 39–49. @2010 GALA.
OECD. (2012). Programme for International Assessment (PISA). *Results from PISA 2012.*
Planned Parenthood. (2013). Pregnancy and childbearing among U.S. teens. https://www.plannedparenthood.org/files/PPFA/pregnancy_and_childbearing.pdf.
Ritz, B., & Wilhelm, M. (2008). Air pollution impacts on infants and children. *Southern California Environmental Report Card-Fall 2008.* UCLA Institute of the Environment and Sustainability. www.environment.ucla.edu/reportcard/article1700.html.
Rivers, J. C., & Sanders, W. L. (2002). Teacher quality and equity in educational opportunity: Findings and policy implications. *Teacher Quality,* 13–23.
Rowe, C. (2014, January 1). How much do dropouts cost us? The real numbers behind pay now or pay later. *The Seattle Times, Education Blog.* http://blogs.seattletimes.com/educationlab/2014/01/03/how-much-do-dropouts-cost-us-the-real-numbers-behind-pay-now-or-pay-later/.
Suglia, S. F., Gryparis, A., Wright, R. O., Schwartz, J., & Wright, R. J. (2008). Association of black carbon with cognition in a prospective birth cohort study. *American Journal of Epidemiology.*
Shonkoff, J. P., & Phillips, D. A. (2000). *From neurons to neighborhoods: The science of early childhood development.* Washington, DC: National Academy Press.

Part II

SUCCESS AND FAILURE

Chapter 4

Failure for the Masses

Bruce S. Cooper

This chapter gives the big, national (and at times, the international) picture of the United States and its K–12 educational standings, failings, and decline in school outcomes over the last decade, as well as the effects of the quality of education on children's health, future educational opportunities, and family income in America.

The view is national, international, in-depth, and longitudinal, as the *changing* "powers of education" are reviewed and analyzed on a "national—comparative international—scale." For recent studies, school systems in the United States ranked our country worldwide in about the fiftieth percentile (in the middle) in effectiveness in educating students.

For example, Molinar (2014) reports in *EdWeek Market Brief*

> The U.S. ranks 19th out of 30 countries in the outcomes it gets from its investments in education, according to "The Efficiency Index: Which Education Systems Deliver the Best Value for the Money?" a report released Thursday by GEMS Education Solutions, a London-based education consultancy.
>
> Finland, Korea, and the Czech Republic were deemed the most educationally efficient countries in the study, which is based on 15 years of data from member countries of the Organization for Economic Cooperation and Development. (p. np)

Inequity of funding and thus "insufficient levels and mean amounts," teacher quality, and mandated standard benchmarks for all students, have together placed the United States in a lower ranking internationally. The failure of the current system to address the needs of children and families in lower socioeconomic areas of the country has ignored the research associated with cognitive functioning and principles for success. We now examine some of the issues around national education quality and its effects on students and society.

We know that education quality is as follows: (1) a resource for students to progress and improve their socioeconomic status through job preparation; (2) a restriction if the children get a poor education, drop out, and cannot progress; and (3) a condition and cause of poverty that are often associated with poor neighborhoods and less than effective schools. Thus, being poor often means living in poor neighborhoods and attending poor schools.

And as we discussed in our earlier book, *Intersecting of Children's Health, Education and Welfare* (2012), being poor also often means less effective health care; along with poorer, less adequate, equitable education; and fewer chances in life of earning a good income. The connections are clear, as we explained:

> Children need more than just good schooling: they require safe lives, good health, and sufficient resources to live and grow successfully in their community. This book makes this vital connection, as society must promote a quality education, available health services, and financial equity and opportunity for all. (Nielsen Book Data)

Thus, these needs are important for all. For as we improve the education "of the masses," this will help them and the country economically, and may mean becoming a healthier nation and community. If more people can afford to live in a better community, send their kids to better schools, receive better health care, everyone's lives will improve. In effect, children brought up in poor homes and neighborhoods are more likely to get a poor and limited education, have problems finding good jobs, and therefore often cannot get their kids improved education.

One affects and relates to the other: education, income, health, and life, are all interconnected, as this book shows. And how do societies break the connections, improving education, jobs, income, health, and family well-being? We will look mainly at better education, as a key means for improving life, income, health, and general welfare. Not an easy task.

SEVEN KEY ISSUES ON SCHOOLS' MASS FAILURES

We now explore seven indicators of both the power of education and the mass dangers and effects of poor education on our children, on their economic lives and futures, and on our nation as a whole. The first issue is about recruiting, training, supporting, and keeping teachers, as they are critical to the children's lives and education.

1. Teacher Training, Retention, and Quality

The Hechinger Ed blog has reported that most US teachers (of math) go to the best colleges for training, although sadly, the poorest college programs produce most of the nation's teachers, and the results are predictable:

> The United States has some of the best university-based math teacher training programs in the world. But we also have some of the worst—and those poorest performing programs produce 60 percent of the country's teachers in schools with the highest percentage of students living in poverty, according to research released earlier this month from William Schmidt, co-director of the Education Policy Center at Michigan State University. The United States was the only country in this study to have such a wide range of performance by math teachers in teacher preparation programs (Asif, 2013, p. 1), as reported.

The Teacher Education Study in Mathematics (TEDS-M), for example, is an international analysis, focusing on the preparation of teachers of mathematics at the elementary and middle school levels. In the United States, the focus has been extended to include future high school mathematics teachers. The research is a project of the International Association for the Evaluation of Educational Achievement (IEA), the agency that sponsors cross-national studies including the Third International Mathematics and Science Study (TIMSS). This project (TEDS-M) builds on the results of TIMSS and breaks new ground as the first large-scale international study to examine how teachers are prepared to teach.

Mathematics is but one vital subject that students need to master and excel at. It has easy international comparisons, since math is math across the world. Remember that $2 + 2 = 4$ in every classroom and nation worldwide, even in the United States. Until the United States improves its teaching and standing in math, masses of kids are being affected. The Common Core, across the states, is a good means for examining the test results and standards for US schools. For as the Common Core State Standards (2015) explains:

> For more than a decade, research studies of mathematics education in high-performing countries have concluded that mathematics education in the United States must become substantially more focused and coherent in order to improve mathematics achievement in this country. To deliver on this promise, the mathematics standards are designed to address the problem of a curriculum that is "a mile wide and an inch deep."
>
> These new standards build on the best of high-quality math standards from states across the country. They also draw on the most important international models for mathematical practice, as well as research and input from numerous sources, including state departments of education, scholars, assessment developers, professional organizations, educators, parents and students, and members of the public. (p. 11)

And teachers have often been slow to learn, adopt, and use technology in their classrooms, with students often "ahead" of teachers in the hi-tech world. It is sad because we see engaging devices that put the world at their class's fingertips, as these twelve useful suggestions are made, even for "technophobic" teachers (Haynes, 2015).

Perfect Ed Tech Activities for Beginners

- *Do a PowerPoint "Game Show Review."* Many tech-savvy teachers have used Microsoft PowerPoint to create review games based on famous game shows. . . . [It's a] fun way to practice using a projector and get your students to review important material.
- *Have students complete a written classroom activity as if it was online.* Ever have your students write a diary from the perspective of a character or famous person? . . . With the Web 2.0 world, [learn about the person and imagine what a day in his/her life might be like] which can be a great first step.
- *Try a Webquest.* A webquest guides students to search the Internet for specific information. [An interested teacher could give a general assignment with specific questions and issues, and ask students to query the Internet for answers. The students could then make a presentation to the class on their findings, thus using tech together to find, write up, and present the results.]
- *Use technology as a topic for a writing assignment.* For younger students, have them write a "how-to" piece about using technology in the classroom." It's a natural fit, as young people usually have a higher comfort level with technology than many adults. Tell kids to write a piece instructing someone—maybe a grandparent?—on how to send an email, set up an iPod, or play a video game. For older kids, have them research the impact technology has had on a particular time in history or science or include a unit on science fiction and technology in your Language Arts curriculum.
- *Create a class webpage.* A class webpage can be anything from a basic site where you post announcements (think about an "online bulletin board") to a much more elaborate one that includes class photos, a class blog, downloadable materials, and your own domain name. [For those just starting out, try Scholastic's free Home Page Builder.]
- *Use an online grading system.* While some schools are mandating the shift to web-based grade books, you don't have to wait to try one out. Sites like MyGradebook.com (http://www.mygradebook.com) offer the opportunity to track grades, record attendance and seating charts, and compile reports on student progress. You can also email students and parents directly to allow them to view their updated grades.
- *Do an email exchange.* When we were kids, some teachers had class penpals or had you practice your penmanship by writing a letter to an author.

Failure for the Masses   45

[Introduce the twenty-first-century version of that by assigning an email exchange.] Have your students exchange emails with students in another school, city, state, or country—especially valuable if both sets of students are studying the same material.
- *Give multimedia presentations—or have your students give them.* Liven up a traditional lecture by using a PowerPoint presentation that incorporates photographs, diagrams, sound effects, music, or video clips. For high school teachers, consider having students develop presentations as a review tool before semester exams. Their work may be so good that you will want to use it in future classes!
- *Supplement your lessons.* When you've taught the same material for a while, you—and your students—may find it less-than-exciting. A quick Internet search may help you identify ways to supplement your lessons with interesting new material.
- *Create a class blog or wiki.* Take appropriate precautions for Internet safety, but a class blog or wiki can be a great way to integrate technology in the classroom and develop student knowledge. Some teachers use blogs to drive outside-of-class discussion—particularly helpful for AP/IB students who are motivated but short on class time.
- *Listen to—and/or create—a Podcast.* There are thousands of podcasts available on the Web. Search for ones that meet students' needs. Some colleges are offering professors' lectures via podcast, which can be great for advanced students.
- *"Publish" your students' work.* Tools exist today to allow students to create really professional looking work using a desktop computer. Have students create a short film, run an ongoing class website that features student work and opinions, or—if they're really ambitious—raise the money to have their work professionally published by a self-publishing company like iUniverse or Lulu.

No matter what your skill level, integrating technology in the classroom offers the chance to increase student interest and teach valuable professional skills—and have some fun! (Haynes, 2015)

Mass electronics exist to help improve mass education for all.

2. Student Graduation Rates and Dropouts

Other important measures of education and its effectiveness are the levels and percentage of students who graduate, versus those who do not—and are "dropouts." Data in the United States, collected by the Office of School Superintendent of Public Instruction, show both the overall rate of graduation as well as the rates for various ethnic groups (Dorn, 2013). The latest data show the following:

> The adjusted four-year cohort graduation rate is 77.2 percent for the class of 2012. Asian students have the highest graduation rate (84.4 percent). They are followed by White students (80.4 percent), students identified with Two or More Races (78.1 percent), Black students (67.1 percent), Hispanic students (66.7 percent), Pacific Islander students (64.5 percent), and American Indian students (56.8 percent).

Thus, about a quarter of all students, regardless of race or ethnic background, failed to graduate high school, with the highest group of dropouts being the Native Americans (with only about 57 percent graduating). Asian (80.4 percent graduating) and white (80.4 percent) Americans graduated at higher but still fairly low levels, given the importance of a high school diploma for getting jobs, making livings, and living a quality life. Diplomas are symbols of power in modern life.

3. College Applications and Admissions

The Teacher Education Study in Mathematics (TEDS-M) is an international study focusing on the preparation of teachers of mathematics at the elementary and middle school levels. In the United States, the focus has been extended to include future high school mathematics teachers.

The research is a project of the International Association for the Evaluation of Educational Achievement (IEA), the agency that sponsors cross-national studies including the Third International Mathematics and Science Study (TIMSS). This project builds on the results of TIMSS and breaks new ground as the first large-scale international study to examine how teachers are prepared to teach.

4. Science Results and Quality

No K–12 subject is more important in life and future careers than the sciences, with a likely carryover into college and beyond. Whether a student seeks to be a medical doctor, nurse, psychologist, or dentist, children in the United States fail compared to kids in other countries. As *Scientific American* explained:

> Americans have grown accustomed to bad news about student performance in math and science. On a 2009 study administered by the Organization for Economic Co-operation and Development, 15-year-olds in the U.S. placed 23rd in science and 31st in math out of 65 countries. On last year's Nation's Report

Card assessments found only one third of eighth graders qualified as proficient in math or science. Those general statistics tell only a piece of the story, however. There are pockets of excellence across the U.S. where student achievement is world-beating. Massachusetts's eighth graders outscored their peers from every global region included, except Singapore and Taiwan, on an international science assessment in 2007. Eighth graders from Minnesota, the only other U.S. state tested, did almost as well. (2012, p. 3)

5. Foreign Language Learning

American students appear to have little incentives or real opportunities in life to learn a "foreign language" in school. True, Latino children and other immigrant children learn English while using their native languages at home and in their communities; but many American kids feel no real need to master another language. The power of knowing and using a second (or even a third) language is not always recognized and may affect students later on, when they travel, mingle, and get to know folks from other countries speaking languages other than English.

6. Public School's Failures, Loss of Funding, Oversized Class, and "Inclusion" without Preparation and Support

Poor schools for poor children are ignored, are being resegregated, and are failing. Health care is rarely easily available to the poor, and we often find pollution in communities and schools. Sadly, we often witness a lack of support and quality of early childhood education. And we witness failure to help English Language Learners (ELL students) assimilate into the American society and schools. Low community support for families is also a problem for the latest immigrants, mainly now from Latin America.

7. Obsessions with Standardized Testing

"Test prep" obsessions are limiting the ability of children to problem solve, think critically, and work creatively. Everything is testing and more testing. But how does this help students learn and teachers teach?

IMPACT OF EDUCATION QUALITY ON STUDENTS' FUTURE LIVES

As we found and discussed in our earlier book, *Intersections of Children's Health, Education, and Welfare* (2012), the effects of education are important and profound, as education opens doors to better jobs, higher income, and access to better health care. This equation is particularly true in the United States with its deep roots in capitalism, where income is critical. Higher income means better housing, schooling, and medical care.

Personal Health and Life Expectancy

We know that income affects health care, particularly in the United States because so much of the health services are part of an individual's employment, as a "fringe benefit." For unemployed, or underemployed people, health services are often only available if they have time and effort to stand on line at emergency rooms or clinics, or try to treat the illness themselves at home. And children from before birth are often severely deficient for poor mothers, in many cases. And seriously, many poor mothers are among the worst served.

According to Smith and Egger (1993), "The limited data that exist on cross national comparisons of inequalities in income and inequalities in health suggest that the two covary. Furthermore, both cross sectional and time series analyses indicate that, for a given overall prosperity, countries with smaller differentials in income experience lower infant mortality and longer life expectancy."

As Smith and Egger further explain: "Exactly those groups who have been subjected to cuts in—or reduced access to—benefits, to casualisation of work, to unemployment, and to changing tax policy, have now been taken to task for their predicament" (1993, p. 2).

Smith and Egger conclude that income has an effect on medical care and well-being, with the "health-wealth" interrelationship for families and their children: "Inequitable distribution of wealth may, therefore, be detrimental to the overall health profile of a country, not just to the health of an increasingly poor and disenfranchised minority" (1993, p. 4).

Personal Income

Family incomes are critical in determining life quality, living arrangement, health care, and local education. Poor families strike out in all areas, with low incomes, poor health care, and less opportunities for their kids' education, based on where they can afford to live and pay property tax (higher in richer communities).

Future Education for the Family

Perhaps the strongest predictors of one generation's learning and prosperity are the level and quality of their parents and grandparents' education, preparation, and financial levels of living, including where and when they can move into better neighborhoods with better schools.

Life and Death of Groups

Even life and death are related to income, class, and well-being and quality of life. As George D. Smith explained:

> When some commentators attempt to reduce higher death rates among manual classes to "cultural patterns of behaviour" such as smoking and diet, they seem to lose sight of this fact. Inequalities in health were considerable at a time, when, if anything, it was better off people who smoked, consumed a higher fat diet, and engaged in little physical activity. Any increasing social polarization of such activities may exacerbate the gradients of health differentials; they are not however their root cause. (p. 1086)

So this chapter has worked to relate life and well-being to social class, education, health, and perhaps, overall, most significantly, to *income*. While more socialist societies may have less economic incentives and paybacks, these nations are organized to provide accessible health services and support to all. More capitalist, entrepreneurial countries, while they have often more vigorous investments economically, give less help to the poor, immigrant, and less educated families and people.

In conclusion, we see the power of education, where students who do well are more likely to find good employment, better housing and schooling for their children, and better health care. As Smith (from the UK) and Egger (from Switzerland) explained so well about life in the UK:

> This sits uneasily with Mr. Major's vision of a classless society, brought about by social mobility and "the capacity of everyone to have the help necessary to achieve the maximum for their ability. With regard to allowing everyone the opportunity of achieving the maximum health—the "be all you can be" so beloved of health promoters—a reversal in the dramatic upwards redistribution in wealth is what is required. (Smith & Egger, 1993, pp. 2–3)

REFERENCES

Asif, A. (2013, October 30). Research suggests poor quality of teacher training programs in U.S. compared to other countries. *Hechinger Ed* [blog].

Cooper, B. S., & Mulvey, J. D. (2012). *Intersections of children's health, education, and welfare.* New York: Palgrave-Macmillan.

Common Core State Standards. (2015). *Preparing America's students for success.* Washington, DC: Common Core State Standards Initiative.

Dorn, R. I. (2013). *Report to the legislature: Graduation and dropout statistics annual report 2011–12.* Washington, DC: Office of State Superintendents of Public Instruction.

Haynes, K. (2015). *12 easy ways to use technology in the classroom, even for technophobic teachers.* TeachHub.com. http://www.teachhub.com/12-easy-ways-use-technology-your-classroom-even-technophobic-teachers.

Molinar, M. (2014, September 4). U.S. "education efficiency" ranks in bottom 50 percent, study says. *EdWeek Market Brief.* https://www.marketbrief.edweek.org/marketplace-lc-12/us_education_efficiency_ranks_in_bottom_50_percent_study_says/.

Schmidt, W. (2013). *On core math standards.* Education Writers Association. http://www.ewa.org/blog-educated-reporter/william-schmidt-common-core-math-standards.

Scientific American. (2012). *U.S. should adopt higher standards for science education, 307*(2), 1–3.

Smith, G. D., & Egger, M. (1993, October 30). Socioeconomic differentials in wealth and health: Widening inequalities in health—the legacy of the Thatcher years. *British Medical Journal, 307*(6912). htttp://www.ncbi.nlm.nih.gov/pmc/articles/PMC1679151/pdf/bmj00045-0005.pdf.

Chapter 5

The Reality of Poverty and Neglect

Janet D. Mulvey

A June 20, 2015, report in *The Economist* cites the reality of the consequences of poverty, lack of education, and unpreparedness for employment. "With less than 5% of the world's population, the US prison population is: five times Britain's, nine times Germany's and fourteen times Japan's" (p. 4). The loss to the nation's bottom line both economically and socially is a story to be told and understood by educators, policy makers, and politicians.

The cost to the American taxpayer for a year of imprisonment is, on average, $31,286 per year, per inmate, reported by Henrichson and Delaney (2012). The average cost of educating a student nationwide is $10,667, according to Barshay (2015) from data released by the National Center for Education Statistics (NCES). This cost is a 2.8 percent drop from the spending in the years 2010–2011 (p. np).

Who are these prisoners, what are their crimes, and how did they become one of the statistics?

This chapter looks into the history of those in impoverished situations, their early beginnings, education, and the policies that remand them in environments where escape is exception to the rule.

THE RISK FACTORS

The latest (2012) national data set for high school graduation rates reveals some interesting demographics. Those who live in more suburban areas in states such as Vermont, Wisconsin, Nebraska, and New Hampshire have graduation rates in the 86–88 percentile, while those in the District of Columbia, New Mexico, and large urban areas graduate at a rate of 50 percent (NCES, 2012).

What is the difference? Do we really believe, given the hard data, that one size fits all? The needs of communities are vastly different based on economic opportunities and quality of educational background. In a study done by the Bureau of Economic Analysis, inequality is growing between those with access to community services and education and those without the same quality of resources (cited in Knoll, 2014).

The politics of catering to the more affluent for votes and government tenure has placed a burden on those with less voice, struggling to make ends meet and living in less than healthy conditions. The severe segregation among public schools in large urban areas underscores the lack of equality in every aspect of daily living.

In a report by Williams (2014), school choice offered by former mayors Bloomberg and Cuomo (current governor of New York State), increasing budgets for charter schools to promote better opportunities for disadvantaged youth, is a myth. First, charter schools cannot take all applicants; thus a random selection is held, leaving many within their public school. Second, allowing students to choose any school within a certain geographical creates the same disbursement issue . . . how many children can one school hold?

Appealing to the populace does not solve the problem of providing excellence in our public schools. Taking funding from the majority of students in public schools and sending messages of blame and incompetence do nothing to address the real problems. Politicians and policy makers must begin to listen to educators, community leaders, and parents to start the healing and improvement for all students attending public schools. Our nation's future depends on it.

POVERTY IN US PUBLIC SCHOOLS

A January 29, 2015, CNN News report on the growing poverty problem in America revealed a troubling trend that "the majority of children in America's public schools now are low income. And that has major implications for the future of the nation's workforce" (Luhby, 2015).

And according to the Poverty and Inequality Report of 2014 by Stanford University, "the rate increased from 12.5 percent in 2007 to 15.0 percent in 2012; and the child poverty rate increased from 18.0 percent in 2007 to 21.8 percent in 2012" (p. 5). The rise continues as skills for meaningful employment increases and the failure of educational attainment, among the poor continues. The report indicates that current statistics maintain the worst numbers of those living in poverty since 2000.

Statistically 90 percent of children still attend public schools with more than 45 percent eligible for free or reduced lunch. And due to mandated curricula that do not take learning differences and needs into account, the proficiency in math and English language arts continues a downward spiral among low-income children.

The diagrams in figures 5.1-1 and 5.1-2 illustrate the proficiency levels of low-income children over a ten-year period. The test scores illustrate the difference between low-income and those who are more affluent.

Children born into low-income or poor families do not begin with the same opportunities as those in the more affluent classes. The accusations of laziness, lack of motivation, and government dependency are simply not statistically correct. The excuse is used by too many uninformed policy makers and politicians in the old blame game rather than reading the research from institutions that are not politically motivated.

Inequality begins at before birth. Prenatal care with proper nutrition and health care are determinants for a healthy birth and proper development. While lasting effects have yet to be determined, it remains a less than quality start to life. According to Pathak and Kapil (2004), "During pregnancy, maternal energy requirements are substantially increased, exacerbating the consequences of an unhealthy or inadequate diet in the mother" (p. 97). Infancy without proper nutrition continues the inadequate spiral toward development.

Nutrition continues to play an important role in health throughout a lifetime. Chronic ailments and diseases have been linked to unhealthy diets. Lower-income families cannot afford the fresh fruits and vegetables at large grocery markets, and neighborhoods where the impoverished reside are often deplete of markets selling healthier foods. Children are affected by poor nutrition over which they have no control and the results are often physical, emotional, and cognitive.

Being born into a family or to a mother living in poverty usually means poor nutrition and environments, and stressful conditions. Developmental delays, physically and cognitively, result in poor beginnings for school readiness. Continued resource inadequacies in schools are condemning our young impoverished children to perpetual unhappiness, stress, and lack of possibility for social or economic mobility. Graham (2015) reports, "In the United States, poverty is exacting a high-cost—not in terms of water and power but in terms of stress, unhappiness and pain" (p. np).

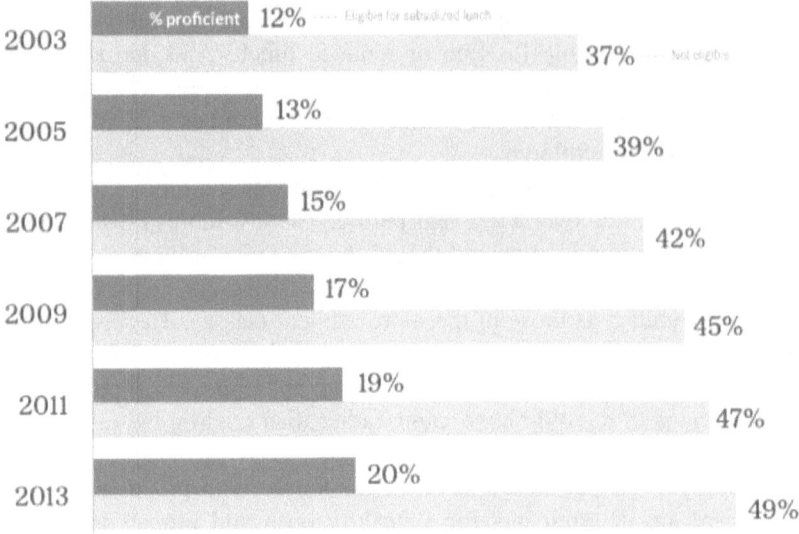

Figure 5.1-1 Reading Scores between Low-Income and those Students from More Affluent Background. *Source*: CNN Money January 29, 2016.

Figure 5.1-2 Reading Scores between Low-Income and those Students from More Affluent Background. *Source*: CNN Money January 29, 2016.

REALITY OF EDUCATING THE POOR

Children entering school for the first time are unable to meet the standards placed upon them in the classroom. They enter with lower cognitive development, less physical well-being, and fewer positive experiences that lend to learning. Some come hungry, ill, and stressed from conditions within families or communities. Their families do not have the advantages of preparing them, often having similar experiences and unable to offer the support necessary for success.

According to Burger (2010), "They enter school with fewer academic skills . . . and lag behind in their cognitive development during the later school years" (p. 141). Consistent failure or underperformance perpetuates the conditions leading to dropping out and being unprepared and without skills to find meaningful and economically supportive work.

Homeless trends for young children have continued to increase, beginning shortly after the great recession of 2008. The homeless count for children has risen by 8 percent since 2012–2013. According to Lesley (2014), "1.3 million homeless children enrolled in preschools and K-12 schools in the 2013–2014 school year and that number grew by an 8 percent increase from the previous year and an 85 percent increase since the beginning of the recession" (p. np).

Educators working in high poverty schools tell us that teaching/learning takes second place to other issues that affect their students. Factors of hunger, illness, cleanliness, and social and psychological problems take up much of their time, often at their own expense.

Government funding targeting the poor and underserved schools and population has not kept pace with the increased needs of students and schools. According to Bidwell from the *U.S. News & World Report* (2014), "Congress has cut K–12 education spending by 20 percent since 2011." The report continues to show the lack of commitment to public education by revealing that funding "has been disproportionately placed on the chopping block by Congress" (p. np).

Inequities in resources, teacher compensation, quality, and unhealthy physical and emotional environments all hamper potential success in school. It seems as though the days of separate but equal facilities—long adjudicated as unequal in the *Plessy vs. Ferguson* case—have been reinstitutionalized in our school system, though not necessarily based on race but on wealth.

Case in point: Neighboring towns in Westchester County, New York, illustrate the hard facts. One of the richest towns in lower Westchester boasts $27,926 per pupil expenditure, 15:1 teacher–pupil ratio, and teacher salaries ranging from $62,000 to $104,000. There is no need for a free lunch program; the median wage is $200,000 for the residents. The neighboring district, in contrast, spends $12,000 per student with a class ratio of 28–30:1 ratio in a classroom. The median household wage is $50,000, a stark contrast to their neighbors. Teachers earn from $46,000 to $74,000 annually. The free and reduced lunch program serves 85 percent of the school population (*Westchester Magazine*, 2013).

Unfortunately, race remains a factor in wealth and educational attainment. People from poor neighborhoods are overwhelmingly black or Hispanic. According to Rothstein (2013), "Racial isolation of African American children in separate schools located in separate neighborhoods has become a permanent feature of our landscape" (p. 2). Less funding, resources, and preventative measures are lacking in early health and preschool intervention.

The two districts cited offer an example of the current segregation phenomena: the wealthier district boasting a population of 87.1 percent white, 1.3 percent black, and 4.4 percent Hispanic; while the less wealthy district has 63 percent black, 12.3 percent Hispanic, and 19 percent white.

Rothstein goes on to report that in neighborhood schools, "African American students are more isolated than they were 40 years ago, while most education policymakers and reformers have abandoned integration as a cause" (p. 2).

The graduation rates between the two districts are vast, 96 percent for the wealthier and 47 percent for the less wealthy district. The disparity between economic factors seems apparent and yet little attention is paid to equalize the opportunity for the students in the less affluent area. Research has provided the evidence through neuroscientific testing focused on brain development, cognitive processing, and language acquisition between and among socioeconomic groups that performance gaps and achievement are directly affected by the wealth of the school district and the community.

NATURE VERSUS NURTURE

The controversy of whether nature or nurture plays the most important role has, for the most part, been put to rest. Psychologists and neuroscientists have determined that both are intertwined into the development and successful growth of an individual.

According to LeDoux (1996), "Research has shown that not only do nature and nurture each contribute to who we are, but also that they speak the same language" (p. 12). The study by LeDoux goes on to impress the importance of both in connecting the nerve cells that help shape experience, learning, and function.

Children brought into environments with more negative than positive experiences learn different skills than those that pertain to a better opportunity for social mobility. The promising information brought to us via twenty-first-century neuroscience is that cognitive functioning can be improved, new connections in the brain can be strengthened, and learning can take place given best practices and developmental learning.

Those who live at or below the poverty line report mental stress, chronic pain, and dissatisfaction with life. They are often unhappy, angry, and express hopelessness. Living in stressful environments, unsure of day-to-day events, prohibits planning for future opportunities. Discrimination due to

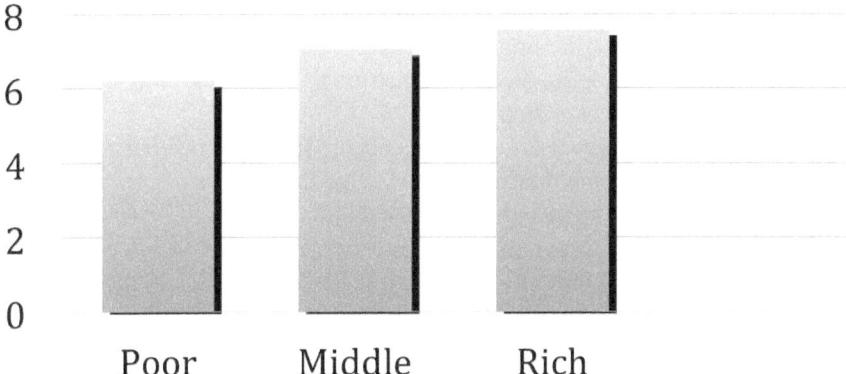

Figure 5.2 Percent of Lower Well-Being Linked to Wealth. Subjective Well-Being Score 0 = Worst, 10 = Best. *Source*: Soumya Chattopadhyay and Carol Graham (2015), using Gallup Healthways survey, in Carol Graham (2015).

impoverished conditions is exposed in Tirado's book, *Hand to Mouth: Living in Bootstrap America* (2014). Ms. Tirado writes about the sexual advantage taken of her while working as a waitress (one of three jobs).

The graph in figure 5.2 shows the ranking (1–10) of well-being in relation to income. As shown, those who live in poverty have a lower level of well-being than their more wealthy counterparts.

Chronic pain, an ailment suffered by many living in poverty, is accompanied with mental fatigue and stress. The pain and hopelessness reduce any motivation to work, learn, or plan for the future. Children born and brought up in these environments have little chance to succeed. Lack of language interaction, inventive play, and social or experiential activities place these young students at a clear disadvantage entering school.

The lack of cognitive development, physical well-being, and social/behavioral skills, mean that children enter with few, if any, academic readiness or expectations. The use of current standardized assessments to determine levels of achievement is a waste of time in measuring growth for underprivileged children. The assessments are another form of punishment, furthering and reaffirming the mental distress that makes them feel unworthy.

Discrimination adds to the feeling of depression and anger as was depicted in 2015 by angry riots in Baltimore, Ferguson, and other cities with large numbers of minority black and Hispanic populations. Segregated schools, poorer quality teachers, and fewer resources exacerbate the negative experiences in education and feelings of inequality. The facts are as follows:

- Income inequality among young adults continues to be greater than any other group, especially for those without a high school diploma.

- Approximately 66 percent black children, compared to 11 percent of white children, are raised in the bottom fifth of the income ladder.
- White families had wealth eighteen times greater than Hispanic households and twenty times greater than black.
- Social mobility to greater wealth status occurs in only 4 percent of those in the bottom fifth income bracket.
- Fifty-three percent of black children raised in the bottom fifth of the income bracket will remain economically depressed compared to 32 percent of white children. (Children's Defense Fund, 2012)

Children living under the conditions of extreme poverty have learned not to expect anything different, that the status quo is the expectation. They have also learned, while perhaps not consciously, that they are invisible by government policies and regulations. The feelings of those living beyond the segregated communities are best told by Carey Fuller, a homeless mother:

> Poverty in this country is not accidental, it's a direct result of funneling wealth upwards to the elite and no one feels that pinch more than the people directly affected by bad policies. It's also policy to under report the true numbers of people living in poverty and the reason behind those policies is politics. Even more exasperating is not knowing when help is going to arrive because some groups get priority status over others, which leads to a lot of frustration due to programs having policy goals to meet. (Fuller, 2013)

Economic disparity is a direct cause of success and failure differences in our public schools. Nature is untested because nurture is an unequal source of opportunity for those living under the stresses of economic despair. Performance gaps cannot be alleviated simply by increasing dollars spent in a community school. Families need both economic and social intervention. Schools need to become the community center for all families. Health care, nutritional counseling, education workshops, and training for employment opportunity are all essential.

Disparity in income and deprivation of resources have resulted in poor academic performance among those in low-income or impoverished communities. According to the OECD, "socio-economic status accounts for 17 percent variation in test scores in the U.S. compared to 9 percent in Canada or Japan" (p. 4). In New York City alone only 18 percent of students in the poorest communities scored above proficiency in math, a poor predictor of readiness for higher education or training for employment.

The question arises, how inequality in income, employment opportunity, and education relate to each other and the effect they have on a child's chance for social mobility. Alan Krueger (2012) addresses the reality of income inequality and labels it the "Great Gatsby Curve." He relates, "The idea behind the curve is that inequality in rental incomes (and other means) will result in even greater inequality for their children" (p. np).

The devastating effect on the future of the American economy is founded on the fact that millions of poor children will be unprepared for twenty-first-century jobs and will rely on the government to subsidize their income. How much better would we be if we provided the means for a quality education resulting in an increase to the gross national product?

POLICY MISCONCEPTIONS

Policies proposed by politicians to help the poor have not been based upon research but on unlikely standards for more wealthy citizens. Understanding the plight of poverty means putting aside political loyalties and learning about what is necessary to break the poverty cycle disease.

Why is it important for local and national governments to listen and learn about poverty? Current beliefs about the causes of poverty have influenced ill-conceived and implemented programs. Thinking that it is easy to break out of poverty is confirmed by a recent political statement from presidential hopeful Marco Rubio: "To succeed in life, you don't just need skills and a good job. You need to have values like hard work, discipline and self-control" (2015). The notion that millions of children are growing up in families "unwilling" to teach proper values is evidence of a complete lack of knowledge of the many facets causing and condemning people to live in poverty.

Being born into poverty is being born into a social institution where invisibility to the political agenda is convenient, where environments are ripe with toxins and chemicals, the importance of health care is debated, and blame for one's poverty is on the individual. The realities of poverty are either ignored or dismissed by those who benefit most from current financial control and wealth.

The free market enterprise so revered by the wealthy here in the United State is a system based upon the basic principle of supply and demand. The argument among advocates is that free market enterprise provides opportunities for distribution of goods and creation of new business to grow and add to the gross national product. The free market proponents also tout the creation of new jobs and opportunities for all Americans.

The intervention of government in the free market enterprises, the critics argue, limits the growth and potential of new and existing markets. The truth is the free market enterprise limits participation by a large section of the population and remains in control of those with the most wealth. Even Alan Greenspan, the former chairman of the Federal Reserve, a conservative Republican and a strong advocate of free markets, has raised concern about the inequality of participation as a threat to the entire system. Greenspan states, "You cannot have the benefits of capitalist market growth without the support of a significant proportion, and indeed, virtually all of the people; and if . . . the rewards of capitalism are being distributed unjustly, the system will not stand" (Komlos, 2015).

CHANGING THE MIND-SET

Policy makers and politicians have difficulty dealing with negative elements in their districts, states, or nationally. The 2015 riots in Baltimore and Ferguson, Missouri, had as much to do about poverty as racial tension. For example, in Baltimore, 22 percent of the residents (black) have no high school education. The income level is below $20,000 annually, and unemployment is 22 percent (way above the national average of 5.3 percent).

So the question among too many politicians is: Why don't they stay in school? Free public education is available to the poor. And according to former US president George W. Bush, everyone can have health care; they can go to emergency rooms.

Enter a school in an impoverished area of Bronx, New York, and observe the condition of the school and search for the resources that support learning. Compare the mandates of government-designed curricula, and then study the readiness of the students' ability to meet those standards. Why aren't they ready and why do they feel defeated?

By the time many impoverished students reach middle school, they have been retained, experienced only failure, and are still expected to follow a curriculum based on obscure subject matter with no connection to their lives.

The reality encompasses the hopelessness surrounding the poor. Stress, worry, inability to cope with the daily struggles, as well as deteriorating neighborhoods, unavailability of services, poor schools, fewer jobs, rising discontent, and crime are all elements to wake up from and go to bed with—without any answers. Krueger (2012) ponders why this is happening and what we can learn from research studies. If income inequality begins at birth, what are the reasons and what should a country like America do about it?

According to Duncan (2015), "The political dimension is clear in poor communities where the haves and the have-nots live in worlds apart, and a few powerful families control jobs and politics" (p. 184).

Socioeconomic status is the driving force in a person's ability to function, physically and mentally. The correlation between success, failure, social mobility, and SES has been documented for years. Behavioral scientists and educational professionals have documented the results for the vast majority of individuals living under the dark cloud of poverty.

As the distance grows between the money classes, the more we, as a society, will suffer from an uneducated and unproductive populace. It is time to listen to the facts and begin the remediation for those who are young enough to benefit from quality education and health care at the least.

According to DeNavas-Walt and Proctor (2015), educational attainment is related to the poverty cycle. "In 2014, 28.9 percent of people aged 25 and older without a high school diploma were in poverty. The poverty rate for those with a high school diploma but no college was 14.2 percent and with some college 10/2 percent" (p. 16).

Understand that poverty is not a choice. It begins at birth and perpetuates into early childhood, adolescence, and adulthood. According to Agin (2010),

> A pregnant woman in poverty looking at you from a doorway of a shack, in Chicago, Georgia or Texas is in a sisterhood with a woman in a shack in West Virginia. The woman may be black, brown or white, but it's a sisterhood. Poverty produces its own culture, its own environment and in most industrialized countries and countries that are now rapidly developing, the culture of poverty. (p. 289)

Breaking the cycle is time-consuming but advantageous to the American society at large. Healthy beginnings with good prenatal care, early childhood schooling, and intervention, quality schooling and education, graduation, employment, and finally the potential to contribute to family, community, and the nation's gross product are the steps necessary to break the cycle.

BREAKING THE CYCLE

Promising information that cognitive levels can be improved by changing environments gives pause for hope. Politicians need to recognize that the increasing rate of those falling below the poverty line is more costly than spending the dollars on better education and health care.

Recognizing the current and future need for a better beginning can offset the damage done by a viral environment—physically, mentally, and educationally. The research cannot be clearer; the earlier the better can offset developmental delays. Environmental toxins are poison to development, and poverty becomes a generational problem where hope is bashed and dependency flourishes.

Without hope for a better day, week, or month, motivation to try is almost impossible. Linda Tirado (2014) explains,

We start the day with a deficit. Most poor people do not wake up feeling refreshed and rested. Poor people wake up knowing that today, no matter how physically shitty we may feel, we cannot call in sick . . . or we have to find something to do with our endless unemployed hours . . . that's all the day is, just another gray nothing. (pp. 57–58)

There can be hope and it starts with education. The vicious cycle can be broken but policy makers need to be on board and part of the solution. Scientific evidence should be the basis of school reform, not policies based on national programs that are delineated along grade levels and rote learning.

Early childhood programs should be tied to government subsidies that not only mandate the program for the child but also include educating the parent. The Abecedarian project of the 1970s is a perfect example of implementing a comprehensive program serving child and parent.

DEVELOPMENTAL VERSUS PRESCRIBED LEARNING

Learning theory is a conceptual framework based on age, culture, environment, socioeconomic status and experiential background. Perhaps one of the better explanations of the relationship between theory and practice is explained by Shuell (2013): "Classroom learning involves social, emotional, and participatory factors in addition to cognitive ones . . . activities in which the student actually engages (mental, physical, and social) determines what is learned in the classroom"(p. 6).

Learning begins at birth but the trajectory is different for all children; and for those who are born into less stimulating environments, learning can lag. Scientific studies confirm that social economic status influences cognitive growth and development of the brain. It is no secret that those who reside in more affluent neighborhoods perform better academically, physically, and emotionally. Scores on standardized tests reflect the affluence and experiential background afforded during their developmental years.

Studies conducted through electrophysiological and neuroimaging have been able to "characterize SES disparities in neurocognitive functions." Areas of language development and executive functioning seem to be the most clearly affected (Loughan & Perna, 2012). Children from lower SES areas score more than two years behind on standardized language tests, resulting in more stress from school leaders to prepare for once yearly tests rather than improve the learning necessary for academic success.

Meeting standards set by government norms, without prior background experience, is setting up a system of failure for millions of children. Expectations without a healthy start physically, emotionally, and/or developmentally are prescriptions for failure. Readiness for school depends on many factors: social and behavioral, oral communication, fine motor development, letter and number recognition, experience with books and stories, and finally parental support.

Evidence speaks loudly: children with poor nutritional and educational starts remain stuck in poor neighborhoods. Children with good/healthy nutrition and education remain in more affluent neighborhoods with the opportunity to succeed.

Assessing needs informally on an individual basis (informal assessment) can determine the needs for each child, developing a program beginning on the assessed baseline, and using standards as goals to improve levels of achievement. Each child meets success on a linear scale, motivating the eagerness to learn more and participate in a rigorous evidence-based classroom.

Rethinking the Title I grants from President Lyndon B. Johnson's administration and spending that money on quality preschools mandated for low-income children and their parents can move the nutrition rate from poor to healthy, provide the language-based authentic programs necessary for school readiness, and give parents training for more reliable and higher paying jobs. The increase in parental potential will support the efforts within this comprehensive program.

SUMMARY

The evidence is clear: children need a healthy start for a successful finish. Good prenatal care, healthy environments, nutrition, developmental readiness, and quality schools are essential for a chance at success in life.

In a study conducted by Pew Charitable Trusts (2012), a measure was taken to determine the social and economic mobility for children based upon their families' status. Measured in quintiles, 43 percent of children "stuck" at the bottom showed little or no opportunity for economic mobility while 40 percent of children whose families were of more affluent means were "stuck" at the top. Thus, according to the 2012 Pew report, "20 percent of parents with the lowest income during their prime earning years are in the bottom quintile, while 20 percent with the highest income are in the top quintile" (p. 3).

Using scientific and economic research and data, policy makers must change the political mind-set to begin the process of developing programs to assist the poor. Quality preschools that use developmental assessments to determine strengths and weaknesses and programs to remediate deficit areas will prepare readiness levels for children entering kindergarten. Daycare facilities that coincide with preschool can offer parents (often single mothers) an opportunity to learn how to support their children and train them for future employable jobs.

Providing safe environments, free from toxins, eliminates many of the chronic ailments suffered by the young, old, and poor. Building or renovating schools to be inviting, resourced, and safe spaces sets a positive, caring tone—motivating the desire to be in attendance and learn. Establishing authentic programs that celebrate culture and diversity engages students while teaching the basics and beyond.

Educating policy makers—local, state, and federal—on the benefits of spending the dollars necessary to bring about change for the poor and underprivileged will result in a healthier, more positive, and productive citizenry contributing to society and the country as a whole.

It is time for our country to come together for the sake of our children, families, and our nation.

REFERENCES

Agin, D. (2010). *More than genes: What science can tell us about toxic chemicals, development, and the risk to our children.* New York: Oxford University Press.

Barshay, J. (2015, February 2). School spending per student drops for the second year in a row. *The Hechinger Report.* hechingerreport.org/19291/.

Bidwell, A. (2014, September 23). Number of homeless students reaches all-time high. *U.S. News & World Report.* http://www.usnews.com/topics/author/allie-bidwell.

Burger, K. (2010). How does early childhood care and education affect cognitive development? An international review of the effects of early interventions for children from different social backgrounds. *Early Childhood Research Quarterly, 25*(2), 140–165.

Children's Defense Fund. (2012). *Portrait of inequality 2012: Black children in America.* http://www.childrensdefense.org/library/data/portrait-of-inequality-2012.pdf.

DeNavas-Walt, C., & Proctor, B. D. (2015). *Income and poverty in the United States: 2014 current population report* (Report No. P60-252). Washington, DC: United States Census Bureau. www.census.gov/content/dam/Census/library/publications/2015/demo/p60-252.pdf.

Djukic, A. (2007). Folate-responsive neurologic diseases. *Pediatric Neurology, 37*(6), 387–397.

Duncan, C. (2015). *Worlds apart: Poverty and politics in rural America.* 2nd ed. New Haven, CT: Yale University Press.

The Economist. (2015, June 20). Jailhouse nation: 2.3 million reasons to fix America's prison problem.

Fuller, C. (2013, July 24). What our reaction to poverty says about us. *Huffington Post.* http://www.huffingtonpost.com/carey-fuller/what-our-reaction-to-pove_b_3645947.html.

Graham, C. (2015, February 19). The high costs of being poor in America: Stress, pain and worry. *Brookings*. https://www.brookings.edu/2015/02/19/the-high-costs-of-being-poor-in-america-stress-pain-and-worry/.

Henrichson, C., & Delaney, R. (2012, February 29). The price of prisons: What incarceration costs taxpayers. VERA Institute of Justice. http://www.vera.org/pubs/special/price-prisons-what-incarceration-costs-taxpayers.

Knoll, S. (2014). Waging war on poverty: Historical trends using the Supplemental Poverty Measure. http://www.journalistsresource.org/studies/economics/inequality/supplemental-poverty-measure-historical-trends.

Komlos, J. (2015, May 4). Income inequality begins at birth and here are the stats that prove it. PBS News Hour. http://www.pbs.org/newshour/making-sense/plight-african-americans-u-s-2015/.

Krueger, A. (2012). *The rise and consequences of inequality in the United States*. Remarks as Prepared for Delivery at the Center for American Progress on January 12 (pp. 1–10). https://www.whitehouse.gov/sites/default/files/krueger_cap_speech_final_remarks.pdf.

LeDoux, J. E. (1996). *The emotional brain*. New York: Simon & Schuster.

Lesley, B. (2014, November 10). 1.3 million children should not be left homeless. *Huffington Post*. www.huffingtonpost.com/bruce-lesley/13-million-children-shoul_b_6127784.html.

Loughan, A., & Perna, R. (2012, July). Neurocognitive impact for children of poverty and neglect. *American Psychological Association*. https://apa.org/pi/families/resources/newsletter/2012/07/neurocognitive-impacts.aspx.

Luhby, T. (2015, January 29). The growing poverty problem in America's schools. CNN Money. http://money.cnn.com/2015/01/29/news/economy/poverty-schools/.

OECD. (2012). Country Note: United States: Programme for International Student Assessment (PISA). Results from 2012. (pp. 1–9).

Pathak, P., & Kapil, U. (2004). Role of trace elements zinc, copper and magnesium during pregnancy and its outcome. *Indian Journal of Pediatrics*, *71*(11), 1003–1005.

Pew Charitable Trusts. (2012, July). *Pursuing the American dream: Economic mobility across generations*. Washington, DC: The Pew Charitable Trusts.

Rothstein, R. (2013, August 27). For public schools, segregation then, segregation since. *Economic Policy Institute*.

Rubio, M. (2015). The third Republican debate transcript, annotated. October 28, 2015. https://www.washingtonpost.com/news/the-fix/wp/2015/10/28/the-third-republican-debate-annotating-the-transcript/.

Shuell, T. (2013, July 19). Theories of learning. Education.com. http://www.education.com/reference/article/theories-of-learning/.

Stanford University. (2014). The poverty and inequality report. *Pathways*. http://inequality.stanford.edu/sites/default/files/Pathways_SOTU_2014.pdf.

Tirado, L. (2014). *Hand to mouth: Living in bootstrap America*. New York: Penguin Group.

Williams, P. (2014, March 31). Separate and unequal: The real reasons New York has the county's most segregated schools. *The Daily Beast*.

Part III

SUMMARY OF U.S. AND INTERNATIONAL EFFORTS TO INCREASE EDUCATIONAL OPPORTUNITY AND MOBILITY

Chapter 6

Changing the Landscape
Reinventing Public Education
Janet D. Mulvey

The evidence is clear: public education is failing to produce results necessary to compete internationally, create environments for social mobility, or to maintain citizenry knowledgeable to sustain a democracy.

The United States is continuing to fall behind, as evidenced by our standing on the PISA, the dropout rate from high schools, the increase of children living in poverty, the rate of imprisonment, and generational patterns living in segregated communities with little or no social or economic mobility.

Educational failure continues to be the trend due, in part, to a complete lack of understanding of cognitive development and readiness to learn. Inflexible mandated standards, prescribed rote-style teaching, poor resources, and fewer qualified teachers have become the mantra for the public school. Recent studies on educational failure are compared to the many trials and failures among companies involved in experimental research.

As Jacob (2015) clarifies, "Interestingly the high failure rate for well-designed studies in education is similar to the rates in other fields, including late stage clinical trials in pharmaceuticals and testing in business" (p. np). For-profit companies (when conducting trials) can throw out failures and begin anew. The only loss is to the expected and planned-for expense ratio, knowing that when success is reached, the profit will be greater than the loss.

Experimenting with unresearched, policy-driven educational curricula in a one-size-fits-all format contradicts every proven theory of learning and results in failure for millions of children in the United States. Educating the populace should not be viewed as a business where the profit/loss ratio is the measure for success. The current mandates of measurement are, however, aligned with the business model. And we are suffering increasing losses to the bottom line: our children and our future. We cannot, as a proclaimed democracy, experience the same loss for our country.

Are we reverting back to Plato's philosophy of rule? Okpala (2009) reflects, "History provides examples of autocrats who brought tragedy and devastation to the people that they governed. Many were appointed in an attempt to bring relief in times of turmoil, but ended up by using their political prowess to dictate and oppress" (p. 50).

The demographics of the public school has changed. Fifty-one percent of children attending public school were once "minority" (nonwhite), but are now the majority. Today, students are more culturally diverse, speak languages different from English, and more often than not live under the umbrella of low income. Policy makers thwart support efforts for public schooling by using vague language: school choice, taxpayer dollars for private and religious education, and charter schools to divert money from public schooling that "dictates and oppresses" millions of those attending.

Inequality in environments, school resources, teacher quality, living conditions, and political representation are relegating back to the period reflected in Plato's philosophy of remanding power to the professional elites.

The United States, under Horace Mann, understood the value of educating its entire people. His philosophy established the public school to assure an educated populace that would sustain a democratic system.

Today, the political agenda to support the public school is skewed and support from government has become policy to reward the more affluent and reduce support for the less fortunate. The philosophy of free and appropriate education, while remaining free for all, largely ignores the appropriate part.

This chapter focuses on how to reinvent public education and change the landscape through policy, politics, leadership, and researched practices that serve all children residing in the United States.

LEADERSHIP: POLITICAL AND EDUCATIONAL

Political

Political leadership nationally and locally must begin to educate themselves on their purpose in representing all the people for the good of the country. Democracy depends on citizen participation regardless of income status. Education is an imperative for participation in the political process. Schooling educates students to become more civic minded through understanding how a government affects their lives, both personally and societally.

The current US political agenda has little to do with equitable opportunities or motivation toward assuring opportunity for those within the lower socioeconomic strata. The result can potentially be catastrophic for the country as a whole. Glaeser, Ponzetto, and Shleifer (2007) explain the correlation between education and civic participation: Educated people become more knowledgeable about political processes and participate more actively through voting, protesting, and participating. Glaeser et al. state "we present some old and new facts about education and democracy. We show that more educated democracies are more stable than less educated ones" (2007, p. 3).

Earlier studies conclude that civic mindedness is developed in the very early years in school. Academic basics are just one part of the standard for success in society. The ability to socialize, compromise, communicate, and collaborate is as important as getting an A in math. California's Department of Education set one content standard that "students understand the obligations of civic-mindedness, including voting, being informed on civic issues, volunteering and performing public service, and serving in the military or alternative service" (Glaeser et al., 2007, p. 11).

Democracy requires broad support from its citizens, understanding the critical issues supporting economic stability, military strength, and societal cohesiveness. The education of all people enhances and strengthens the democratic process, assuring leaders are attending to the needs of the country as an entirety.

Recent events dictate that national, state, and local leaders attend to the needs of its constituents. Protests over unequal treatment by law enforcement, lack of representation in courts of law, mass shootings, increased poverty, and lack of opportunity all equate to segments of society increasingly feeling marginalized. History and research contend that increased disenfranchisement leads to frustration and revolt.

Leaders in positions of power must examine, without prejudice, the events that cause physical disobedience and use the causes to develop policies to correct them. Communities must be restored to, at the very least, healthy and safe places to reside. Education, as the basis for improving opportunity, requires examination from a scientific, historical, and research-based perspective.

Improvement in leadership knowledge, without partisan prejudice, improves the prospects for increasing human capital to its fullest potential. Attending to the causes of poverty from the health and education point of view can begin the process toward recovery for future generations. Political support without curricula mandates can provide the policy backing necessary for all to meet educational standards.

Educational

Superintendents, principals, and local boards of education are responsible for determining a vision suited to the community and school district. Visions and mission statements must be appropriate for the demographic, economic strata, and culture attending their schools. Lofty messages with no connection to the needs of a community become political verbiage with little or no possibility for success.

Moving beyond the political mandated assessments, professional leaders develop programs suited to the community they serve. Informal assessments, to determine baselines of knowledge, are used to develop programs with attainable goals. Students experiencing success become more motivated to learn and progress toward the standard goals mandated by tests.

Leaders in schools are communicative with their families and provide workshops to help parents understand the curricula and become resources for needs they might have. Great leaders make their schools comfortable and inviting places—a community center available to families' interests.

Understanding the culture and seeking input from the community are steps in developing initiatives supporting the learning needs of students, teachers, parents, and local leaders. Examining data from previous assessments and applying researched methodologies create a personalized approach that can be measured for individual and school-wide improvement.

Teachers are supported and validated in their efforts: part of a collaborative team working together with the leadership to develop expertise in implementing researched-based methodologies and rejoicing in results.

Professional educational leaders understand the need to comply with mandates but seek more authentic teaching and learning methods initiating the critical and problem-solving skills necessary for success in real life. Students given the opportunity to experience success, given tasks to stimulate critical thinking, and assessed accordingly will be more engaged, motivated, and better prepared to take and pass mandated tests.

Perhaps one critical attribute for schools leaders is investment in education as the ways and means for the individual to become an upstanding, informed citizen ready to contribute to themselves, their family, community, and society. School leaders have one of the most important professional obligations, to prepare students for every professional, service, and/or trade-related position. Without school leaders, education would be the proverbial "boat without a paddle."

FUNDING

Improving the condition of our current public schools, especially in low-income areas, requires examining and changing the funding structure of our government. The tax base employed to fund education is inherently unequal. Areas of high wealth, while taxed higher, spend much more for the education than those who reside in low-income neighborhoods.

Creating school communities concentrates and combines government, making funding possible to provide counseling, family services, adult education—in addition to curricula for students attending the public school. Relationships between the community and school can build lasting partnerships and help support the educational agenda for students.

Many government programs are outdated and unnecessary, or politically motivated and must be identified and reformed. For example, as reported by Reidl (2009), "Washington spends $25 billion annually maintaining unused or vacant federal properties" (p. np). Many of the other expenditures in Reidl's report seem laughable, such as $92 billion on corporate welfare. The "Pentagon spent $998,798 shipping two 19-cent washers from South Carolina to Texas and $293,451 sending an 89-cent washer from South Carolina to Florida" (p. np). Many expenditures we are more familiar with, such as the bridge to nowhere that was disbanded but still receives funding. Reidl exposed fifty programs funded by the government that are wasteful and unnecessary.

A political agenda supporting wealthy lobbyists takes away fair representation of constituents and worthy programs such as education, and applies funding to high donors and PACs (political action committees). Health care, free early childhood programs, low-income housing, toxic-free environments, educational resources, and teacher education are better investments for the future of democracy. Think what those billions of dollars given to influence an agenda, not in the common interest, could do to improve schools for all the nation's children.

Funding to repair existing school buildings, making them welcoming, safe, and pleasant environments, portrays a message of caring and the importance of the students' education. Providing the resources necessary for an effective education is another important aspect of educating students, availing teachers and students alike the tools necessary for a twenty-first-century education.

Training teachers and administration in researched-based methods of assessment and programs will help meet the needs of the community. Meeting these needs will engage and enhance students' learning, success, and prospects for the future.

EARLY CHILDHOOD

Early childhood education, discussed in chapter 3, is crucial for success in elementary through high school. Care given at prenatal, infant, and preschool stages of cognitive development can determine success or failure in education. Scientific studies and neurological imaging have determined that parts of the brain, the prefrontal cortex and hippocampus in particular, are associated in the development of language, attention, and behavioral/emotional regulation. Azma (2013) explains, "By examining the effects of poverty on specific brain systems—low income developing brain exhibits a characteristic pattern of deficits" (p. G-41).

We have examined the stress factors of living in environments that are toxic chemically, physically, and emotionally. Without health care, proper nutrition, lack of safety, and support from parent and community, the child is reared without any of the prerequisites recognized by researchers for reaching milestones necessary for educational and social development.

If we can educate and convince those with change power to understand the imperativeness of educating the new demographic majority attending our public schools, we can improve schooling and increase productivity to the benefit of society as a whole. Being informed of the importance for early years can change policy emphasis to support early childhood education. Given the ability of the young brain to adapt and grow in a positive environment, improved nutrition and preventative health care can remove the almost certain path to failure.

Lipina and Posner (cited in Azma, 2013) reinforce the possibilities for change by altering the environment. "Exposure to enriched environmental conditions is associated with improved cognitive performance. Stimulating, enriching environments can cause positive neuroanatomical changes in several brain regions" (p. G-43).

It is time for educational and neurological research to drive the agenda for change. Investing in early childhood care and education can assure a greater contribution from future citizens, improve the gross national product contribution, and secure our democratic system.

COLLEGE AND UNIVERSITY PROGRAMS

Schools need textbooks, digital programs, and curricula guidelines based on proven strategies and techniques developed for learning needs in diverse communities. Colleges and universities should be the catalysts for knowledgeable development of these practices. Relying on published profit-based companies has proven a disaster for large segments of US schools.

In Texas, according to Jervis (2014), textbooks published by McGraw-Hill and Pearson had so many inaccuracies that were being read by and then tested on students that it raised questions about racial and social bias. "Did Moses influence the Founding Fathers? Textbooks headed for classrooms are misleading, racially prejudiced, and at times, flat out false" (Jervis, p. np).

Using publication companies more interested in profit than truth and/or education needs to be exposed in colleges to seek more authentic research and implementation of curricula and practice. Exposing future educators to successful pedagogical strategies and practices provides opportunities to examine implementation of a variety of approaches. The one-size-fits-all mentality that has left so many children behind can be used to see comparative outcomes affecting students living in diverse environments.

Teacher education programs have fallen into the trap of published "no thought necessary" programs to teach in classrooms. Common Core and standardized testing–based textbooks have taken away the creativity, critical thinking, and problem-solving skills necessary in the twenty-first century and beyond. Teacher education programs, while familiarizing future educators with current trends, need to take a stand and teach a variety of sound pedagogical practices appropriate for use in classroom environments.

Understanding developmental milestones for learning will help create and implement programs geared for success and progression within learning standards. Students ready developmentally will engage in and use age-appropriate materials, experience success, and understand the relevance of the material. Assessments founded on curricula, taught within development milestones, will better gauge mastery and/or need for reinforcement.

Colleges and universities need to engage with the educational research community, adhering to proven practices, based upon scientific, neurological, and demographic data completed with large samples and comparative analysis. Relying on for-profit, closed-door research has proven a disservice to large public school populations. Following publisher promised outcomes, based on commercially driven data, does nothing to enhance teaching in many classrooms. Following rote standards, lessons, and relying on prescribed worded instruction remove any teacher scholarship or skill. Debasing the professionalism of school leaders and teachers is creating school environments without thought to the community they serve.

Colleges and universities should be involved in authentic assessment development so prospective teachers and school leaders can develop informal screenings to determine students' strengths and weaknesses. Developing curricula based upon both state standards and assessed needs promotes initiative, involvement, and restores the professionalism necessary for schools to succeed.

EVERY STUDENT SUCCEEDS ACT

A promising initiative being introduced is supporting the role of research in helping disadvantaged students attending our nation's public schools. Working within particular settings, researchers are functioning within schools and with educators to determine the best approach based upon specific needs of a community. Dynarski (2015) explains, "The dominant approach to studying a question of whether a practice or program improves an education outcome is known as 'effectiveness' research" (p. 3).

The emphasis is on training teachers through workshops, community college education programs, and schools. Instead of punishing poor performance, the objective is to identify the needs and develop a program best suited for success. Dynarski (2015) adds that the act "gives states the responsibility to develop accountability—comprehensive support and improvement plans—that must include evidence-based interventions" (p. 3). There is hope that government funding, which has been sparse, will be able to support this most crucial research project to improve education for those students with the most need.

States now have an opportunity to improve the educational standards and outcomes. Under the ESSA, Every Student Succeeds Act, state education departments will have the responsibility to oversee and manage the quality of their schools. Burnette (2016) writes, "Now state education departments are looking to shift their roles from being primarily compliance officers to taking a greater initiative on innovation" (p. np).

FAMILIES AND EDUCATION

The Every Student Succeeds Act, while focusing on schools, must also help poor communities understand the importance of education for their children. Evidence suggests that respecting the physical environment (making the school an inviting place), involving parents in planning, and providing community services can draw parents in as part of, instead of separate from, the school.

Low-income parents often have fewer resources, working multiple jobs just to get by. The stressors of providing the very basics are time-consuming and fatiguing. Aside from the physical and emotional effects of living day to day, parents have little time to dedicate to support the schooling of their children. A 2015 Pew Research Center survey indicated that "lower-income parents with children younger than 18 find financial instability can limit their children's access to a safe environment and to the kinds of enrichment activities that affluent parents my take for granted" (p. np).

Teachers in low-income schools must understand the culture, needs, and wants of the community. Communicating with the parents of their students in a positive and inviting way helps establish trust and confidence and engages them in support of the students' education. Teachers themselves must be trained in all aspects about the results of poverty and the stress it can cause for families in their school.

Lefgren and Jacob (2007) in a research study on parents' wants in a school found that "in low-income schools where academic resources are scarce, 62 percent of motivated parents are more likely to choose teachers based on their perceived ability to improve academic achievement" (p. 64).

Understanding the desire of parents for a good education for their children, regardless of income, should be a motivating factor for teachers and staff working in less affluent schools. Providing the best and appropriate education for all students involves teacher, educational leader, and family.

Leaders and school officials can engage the community businesses and services by inviting them in as partners in improving the neighborhood, providing services, and perhaps increasing participation and growth. Partnering with community-based health services can promote more parent involvement through educating and providing them with preventative care.

Leaders and teachers should participate in activities outside of school, make themselves visible within the community, attend local events, and establish themselves as part of, not separate from, the community at large. Adult education classes in the evenings or weekends may inspire parents who have not completed their education or wish to acquire more knowledge to become an integral part of the school.

Families are the main support of their children. As research indicates, most poor families are as committed to education as those who are more affluent. The circumstances of their existence cannot be a reason for providing fewer resources, less quality education, or lower expectations.

Following the research, supporting ways to provide the best education possible will offer those on the lower socioeconomic scale an opportunity for mobility and a chance to contribute to society and our nation.

Opportunity is knocking for innovation in education. States can assess the needs of the poorest performing schools and use research-based methods to determine how to advance learning, beginning with those yet to be born, age birth to five years of age, and those already in school, by understanding and assisting communities segregated by income and race through health care.

SUMMARY

To change and reinvent public education will take a coordinated effort among politicians, policy makers, educators, parents, and researchers. The public education system in the United States is in a downward spiral, putting us further behind most other industrialized countries in the world. The era of mandated assessments, government-influenced curricula, and for-profit publishing monopolies must come to an end.

Political leadership and policy makers must understand the consequences of the past and move forward in educating our populace in order to preserve our democracy. Civic engagement, voting, and understanding the principle of leadership comes from educated peoples. Supporting public education without a political agenda can once again represent the majority of society.

Educational leadership must learn to engage and understand proven research to provide appropriate and authentic curricula to its students. No longer should publishing companies dictate what is learned or how it is presented in the classroom. Research, documented information, and the teaching practices aligned to success must be the new mantra for the classroom.

Developmental milestones founded upon neurological, physiological, and emotional research findings must align with the standards and desired outcomes. Critical thinking, problem solving, and authentic learning are the necessities for the twenty-first-century student. Assessments need to centered on progression toward the final objective.

Early childhood programs for children living in low-income and impoverished areas are necessities to assure the cognitive development for language readiness before entering formal schooling. An understanding of the damage perpetrated on children less than five years of age is imperative to change the environments inhibiting normal growth and opportunity to learn.

Colleges and universities must return and engage in teacher education and training programs founded on pedagogical practices that have been proven successful through educational research. Teachers are the future and should be innovative, collaborative experts in supporting programs for a diverse student body.

Public schools demand teacher quality within all areas, the more and less affluent. Assuring equality for resources, class size, and teaching expertise demands funding policies that are based upon need if success is an expected outcome.

Families are the background of a student's life. Schools are an integral part of the community and support families according to need. Low-income families can rely on school services in health care, counseling, adult education programs, and student achievement. Community partnerships can create cohesive environments producing support for schools, businesses, students, and residents providing a safer and friendlier neighborhood.

Every Student Succeeds Act is a promising initiative based upon educational research on the needs of our poorer citizens. Funding and allocation for at least 5 percent of poor school systems in each state recognizes the desperate call for educational change. If successful, the United States has the opportunity to become competitive internationally, retain a stable democracy, and afford the prospect for all citizens the right for social and economic mobility.

REFERENCES

Azma, S. (2013). Poverty and the developing brain: Insights from neuroimaging. *Synesis: A Journal of Science, Technology, Ethics, and Policy, 40*, G-40–G-48.

Burnette, D. II. (2016, January 20). ESSA poses capacity challenges for state education agencies. *Education Week*. http://www.edweek.org/ew/articles/2016/01/20/essa-poses-capacity-challenges-for-state-education.html.

Dynarski, M. (2015). *Using research to improve education under the Every Student Succeeds Act.* Brookings Institute, Evidence Speaks Series, number 17, vol. I, no. 8, December 10, 1–4.

Glaeser, E. L., Ponzetto, G. A. M., & Shleifer, A. (2007). Why does democracy need education? NBER Working Paper No. 12128. Cambridge, MA.

Jacob, B. A. (2015, December 3). Harnessing the value of "failure." *Brookings*. www.brookings.edu/research/papers/2015/12/03-harnessing-value-failure-jacob.

Jervis, R. (2014, November 17). Controversial Texas textbooks headed to classrooms. *USA Today*. www.usatoday.com/story/news/nation/2014/11/17/texas-textbook-inaccuracies/19175311/.

Lefgren, L., & Jacob, B. A. (2007). In low-income schools, parents want teachers who teach. *Education Next*, 7(3), 59–64.

Okpala, O. (2009, Spring). Plato's republic versus modern democracy. *The Neumann Business Review: The Journal of Business & Information Systems*, 49–59.

Pew Research Center. (2015, December 17). *Parenting in America: Outlook, worries, aspirations are strongly linked to financial concerns.* http://www.pewsocialtrends.org/2015/12/17/parenting-in-america/.

Reidl, B. M. (2009, October 6). 50 examples of government waste. Heritage Foundation. www.heritage.org/research/reports/2009/10/50-examples-of-government-waste.

Chapter 7

Educating Communities

Janet D. Mulvey

What can we learn from the research, experiences, and personal examples of school and individuals living and working in groups and communities who have struggled, sometimes failing—and then succeeding—in improving schools? How can we help whole communities, in and around our schools, to provide support and to experience success for their children and themselves? A simple definition of "school community" is "The various individuals, groups, businesses, and institutions that are invested in the welfare and vitality of a public [and private] school, and its community—that is, the neighborhoods and municipalities served by the school" (Glossary of Education Reform, 2015).

The following is a classical description and definition of "community," critical to the discipline of sociology, using classical theories of Joseph R. Gusfield and Emile Durkheim:

> Gusfield (1975) distinguished between two major uses of the term community. The first is the territorial and geographical notion of community e.g.—neighborhood, town, and city. The second is "relational," concerned with "quality of character of human relationship, without reference to location" (p. xvi). Gusfield noted that the two usages are not mutually exclusive, although, as Durkheim (1964) observed, modern society develops community around interests and skills more than around locality. The ideas presented in this article will apply equally to territorial communities (neighborhoods) and to relational communities (professional, spiritual, etc.). (McMillan & Chavis, 1986, p. 11)

This chapter examines the roles, power, and thus the importance of communities in education, at these levels: (a) the national, (b) regional, (c) local community immediately surrounding school, and (d) within the school and classrooms. Schools are thus creatures of their communities and families. For as Anne O'Brien (2012) explained:

> According to the recent "MetLife Survey of the American Teacher," teachers, parents, and students all agree that parent engagement in schools has increased over the past 25 years. Given the role that family engagement plays in not only academic success, but also life success, that is great news. However, the survey also noted that parent engagement remains a challenge for many schools [and parents]. (p. 1)

We begin by defining "community"—and how the concept of community applies to different school groups and locations, for example: (1) *nationally*, as teachers and their unions, administrators, and parent associations are critical; (2) *regionally* in neighborhoods in and around each school; (3) *within the school* among teachers and administrations; and (4) in the *classroom* and *laboratories* among students and their teachers and aides.

We know of a number of possible programs to improve neighborhoods and communities that are underserved or ignored. We explore the possibilities of schooling for parents and their young children in literacy and language development—and include research that attends to the whole child.

The National Education Association (NEA), the largest education association (and labor union) in the United States, explains its views of the critical importance of community in education in *The Power of Family School Community Partnerships: A Training Resource Manual*:

> The National Education Association has long championed the engagement of parents, families, and communities in all its resources, programs, and publications. The need to build and strengthen family-school-community partnerships has emerged as a major challenge in public education. We know that partnerships are essential for helping students achieve at their maximum potential. Most school professionals now realize that the job of educating students cannot be achieved by their efforts alone. Rather, it requires a collaborative effort with families, communities, and other stakeholders. (Gary & Witherspoon, 2011, p. 6)

But first, we want to understand the power and dynamics of a "community," as families often live near each other, work together, and interact—sharing common concerns and seeking to resolve differences in beliefs, desires, and goals. A community can begin when two or more people have a common interest and work together around that belief or concern. Communities have "structure," often both vertically, with educators in charge and lay people under them; or folks can work together collaboratively—horizontally—bringing their personal and group values and needs "to the table." As Scott London (2014) explained:

Collaborative groups, by contrast, are often structured horizontally. Leadership, to the extent that it exists at all, is broadly distributed. Job titles and professional affiliations fade into the background and people derive their influence from having their ears to the ground, from being well-connected in the community, and from being engaged in a multiplicity of projects. Membership usually spans silos and divisions in the community, processes are guided by norms of trust and reciprocity, and communication is more personal, more conversational, more exploratory than in formal settings. (London, 2014, p. 1)

Most communities have both vertical leaders, spokespeople, elected or appointed leaders, and horizontal relationships as members of the community join, participate, and often work together.

FOUR TYPES OF SCHOOL COMMUNITIES

National School Groups

One perspective on communities is *national*—or at least multistate—where members of different job types form their own associations to give themselves a collective identity, voice, influence, and power. Groups like the American Medical Association (AMA) represent the needs of doctors (MDs) across the country; teachers now have the nation's largest, quite powerful, and influential groups, which now often function as "teacher unions." In particular we see that these two union associations—the American Federation of Teachers (AFT) and the National Education Association (NEA)—both have long histories, starting as professional associations and becoming unions when states allowed collective bargaining for public employees. The NEA is the larger of the two associations of teachers, and even, amazingly, now is the largest labor union of all in the nation. The NEA describes itself as follows:

> The National Education Association (NEA) is the largest professional organization and largest labor union in the United States, representing public school teachers and other support personnel, faculty and staffers at colleges and universities, retired educators, and college students preparing to become teachers. The NEA has 3.2 million members and is headquartered in Washington, D.C. with affiliate organizations in every state and in more than 14,000 communities across the nation; it employs over 550 staff and had a budget of more than $307 million for the 2006–2007 fiscal year. Lily Eskelsen García is the NEA's current president. (NEA, 2015)

These two national unions of teachers have also strengthened the voice of teachers, nationally, state-by-state, and locally in the school district and community—giving teachers national and regional/local roles in shaping policies, determining pay and benefits and education curriculum and programs. The two national teacher unions, the AFT and NEA, attempted to merge in 1998, but the NEA voted merging down in New Orleans.

As Cooper (1998) explained: "If preliminary plans come to fruition, the 2.3 million member National Education Association and the 950,000-member American Federation of Teachers, part of the AFL-CIO, will fuse to create the largest single union in the nation." It didn't happen nationally, although as this NEA description explains, NEA-AFT mergers have occurred in several key states:

> In 1998, a tentative agreement to merge was reached between NEA and American Federation of Teachers negotiators, but ratification failed soundly in the NEA's Representative Assembly meeting in New Orleans in early July 1998. *However, five NEA state affiliates have merged with their AFT counterparts.* Mergers occurred in Florida (the Florida Education Association formed in 1998); Minnesota (Education Minnesota formed in 1998), Montana (MEA-MFT formed in 2000), New York (New York State United Teachers formed in 2006) and North Dakota (North Dakota United) formed in 2013. (NEA, 2015)

Opinion is still divided, as Cooper found, about whether teachers are professionals and should not unionize or are workers and should. In his article "Toward a More Perfect Union," Cooper (1998) examines the advantages and disadvantages of the merger between the National Education Association and the American Federation of Teachers, the importance of unity to preserve public education, and the lessening of influence of the rank and file members of the groups.

Thus, the largest professional and labor community in the United States is K–12 teachers, who wield power in policies and programs nationally and in the fifty states. So community can mean collegiality, voice, and influence (if not power), as teachers stick and work together, giving educators considerable voice and power at the national and state levels. Community can mean power, as workers, professionals, and politicians have learned.

Regional Power in Education

The next levels of community in education exist in the states and local districts. Communities of teachers start in the region and often move up to the state. These communities are highly diverse, among and between the fifty states, and across the county. The US Census describes the system as follows: "The U.S. has more than 14,000 public school districts and spends more than $500 billion on public elementary and secondary education each year (combined spending of federal, state, and local governments)." These districts are statewide in Hawaii, but regional and local in most states. They provide the budget and funding for schools, year by year, and "communities" vary, based on wealth, size, and the socioeconomic status (wealth of families) of students.

Schools Working within Communities

We know that, often, communities are everywhere to benefit education, starting outside and around schools. These areas could be small towns, neighborhoods, and even counties that include people who live within the boundaries of the district, pay local property taxes, and send their kids to their "neighborhood schools." While in the rural areas, students may come from miles away, in cities a few blocks may define the "school area," with many students living within walking distance of their school—particularly at the elementary school level. As Joyce Epstein (2014) explains: "While we all know that home, school and community partnerships are important, and most of us even know what quality home, school and community partnerships look like, we often fall flat in one key area: how to get to them" (p. 3).

She suggests those serious about engaging families and communities begin creating an Action Team for Partnerships. That team should include the principal, two–three teachers, two–three family members, and others in the school or community important to the school's work with families—including a counselor, social worker, business partner, and so on, depending on the school context. At the high school level, Epstein believes the team must include at least one or two students.

In summary, theoretically, the importance of community to schools means:

> The general theory is that by including more members of a school community in the process, school leaders can foster a stronger sense of "ownership" among the participants and within the broader community. In other words, when the members of an organization or community feel that their ideas and opinions are being heard, and when they are given the opportunity to participate authentically in a planning or improvement process, they will feel more invested in the work and in the achievement of its goals, which will therefore increase the likelihood of success. (Epstein, 2014, p. 4)

Communities in Schools

Perhaps the most critical community for teachers and kids is their school itself, which is their home away from home, where teachers and administrators often become almost like their families. Each *classroom becomes a living-learning community,* with power to teach students' subjects, behavior, attitudes, and life. According to *Wikipedia,*

A *learning community* is a group of people who share common academic goals and attitudes, who meet semi-regularly to collaborate on classwork. Such communities have become the template for a cohort-based, interdisciplinary approach to higher education. This may be based on an advanced kind of educational or "pedagogical" design.

Community psychologists such as McMillan and Chavis (1986) state that there are four key factors that defined a sense of community: "(1) *membership*, (2) *influence*, (3) *fulfillment of individuals' needs*, and (4) *shared events and emotional connections*. So, the participants of learning community must feel some sense of loyalty and belonging to the group (*membership*) that drive their desire to keep working and helping others, also the things that the participants do must affect what happens in the community; that means, an active and not just a reactive performance (*influence*). Besides a learning community must give the chance to the participants to meet particular needs (*fulfillment*) by expressing personal opinions, asking for help or specific information and share stories of events with particular issue included (*emotional connections*) emotional experiences." (Learning community, 2015)

And as they show, community is important to the funding, support, and vitality of families *and the schools*. The following table from McMillan and Chavis's article helps to illustrate:

Elements of Sense of Community and Their Hypothesized Relationships

I. Membership
   - Boundaries
   - Common Symbol System
   - Sense of Belonging and Identification
   - Emotional Safety
   - Personal Investment
II. Influence
   A. Member openness to influence by community members; power of member to influence the community.
   B. Member need for consensual validation × community's need for conformity = community's power to influence members (community norms).
III. Integration and Fulfillment of Needs
   A. To the degree that communities successfully facilitate person—environment fit (meeting of needs) among members, members will be able to develop sense of community.
IV. Shared Emotional Connection
   A. Formula 1: Shared emotional connection = contact + high-quality interaction.
   B. Formula 2: High-quality interaction = (events with successful closure—ambiguity) × (event valence × sharedness of the event) + amount of honor given to members—amount of humiliation. (McMillan & Chavis, 1986, Table 1)

THE POWER OF COMMUNITY ACTION IN EDUCATION

Given the importance of community at all levels of education, from the White House to the school house, from the president to the school teacher, we can see what parents, politicians, school leaders, and teachers should and must do to give school the power it deserves in every community. Five steps emerge from this analysis:

1. *From the national to the school local levels, educators should work together with families and communities to improve, support, and sustain education for all.* The power of communities is a critical force for school enhancement and improvement, starting at the national level. Societies produce teachers, help train them, and then employ and compensate them. They have become more honored as professionals, or at least paid better.

    The challenge now and in the future is how to harness this power and influence of the US teachers' unions, the National Education Association (NEA), and American Federation of Teachers (AFT), and use that power to improve education. The NEA and AFT should be included in all major efforts and programs for school change and improvement, as allies and power sources when seeking resources and improved programs. Key representatives of these unions as professional communities nationwide should be consulted (not insulted) to get the ideas, perspectives, and forcefulness of the teaching profession. And the sooner the better!

2. *Power of education often may start locally, in the classroom and school building, and rise and resonate to the national government, to the state house, mayor's office, and back down in the school district.* School reformers should realize the availability, power, and role of teachers and other educators, moving from school, to district, to county, state, and ultimately to the federal government. Harnessing this power in education, across district, state, and regional boundaries, is a key way to make education work better for all. Just as President Johnson harnessed federal resources to help children from poor families under ESEA in 1965, we now have another reauthorization, with the NEA advertising for the need of support:

    Ask the Senate to give all students a fair shot

    Right now, the Senate is working on a reauthorization bill for the Elementary and Secondary Education Act (ESEA), also known as No Child Left Behind (NCLB), the cornerstone education law in America. We believe the new ESEA must focus on opportunity for all, ensure more time for students to learn, and empower educators to lead. (NEA, Issues and Action, 2015).

3. *Teachers have power over the lives of children, and should be honored and supported: power to the teacher!* Finally, we cannot give education the power and influence to help children to break out of the relationship between "health, education, and welfare" mainly around family income and "standard of living," without raising the standing, authority, and roles of teachers, making them finally and substantially *professionals*. The common role of being a "semiprofessional" wears thin, and needs to be changed.

Just as doctors and lawyers are granted professional status, roles, pay, and prestige, teachers too need that status to help improve the relationship between education and the health and income of students in their lives. As the National School Board Association explains:

> Join "Friends of Public Education" (FPE) and be ready to act on behalf of public schools. Federal education policy has far reaching effects on your local public schools and students. NSBAC created "Friends of Public Education" to reach beyond local school board community to individuals who are committed to public education. As advocates you will be notified and called upon to act when critical legislation affecting public schools is before Congress. (See more at http://www.nsbac.org/node/166#sthash.KU0inEFQ.dpuf)

SUMMARY

We cannot say enough that is good or effective about the sense, role, and influence of community in schools, families, and life. Families were meant to work with other families, to share ideas, purposes, and resources in rearing and supporting their kids. Here's Shital Shah's response to the question: How are community schools different from traditional public schools?

> We know that too many of our children and families are not getting equal access to the opportunities and supports that are essential for their success. School is a public democratic institution, supported by tax dollars, so it should be the place in our neighborhoods that affords all children and families equitable education and life chances. All schools should be ones that everyone wants to send their children to. These are the opportunities that *every* family and student has the right to access. Community schools address this goal through their approach to school-community partnerships. Traditional schools tend to have a variety of ad hoc community partners working with their students, families, and teachers, with little coordination. In contrast, the infrastructure of community schools allow these partnerships to be intentional, aligned, and focused on results, thus maximizing their effectiveness. (Capers & Shah, 2014, p. 2)

REFERENCES

Capers, N., & Shah, S. C. (2015). The power of community schools. *Voices in Urban Education,* no. 40.

Cooper, B. S. (1998). Toward a more perfect union. *Teacher Magazine,* 9(8), 55–58.

Durkheim, E. (1964). *The division of labor in society.* New York: Free Press of Glencoe. (Original work published 1893).

Epstein, J. L. (2001). *School, family, and community partnerships: Preparing educators and improving schools.*

Epstein, J. L. (2014). *Center for school, family, and community partnerships.* Baltimore: National Network of Partnership Schools.

Gary, W. D., & Witherspoon, R. (2011). *The power of family school community partnerships: A training resource manual.* Washington, DC: National Education Association, Priority Schools Campaign.

Glossary of Education Reform. (2015). *Great Schools Partnership.* http://edglossary.org/.

Gusfield, J. R. (1975). *The community: A critical response.* New York: Harper Colophon.

Learning community. (2015). *Wikipedia.* https://en.wikipedia.org/wiki/Learning_community.

London, S. (2014). Civic renewal. http://scottlondon.com/site/index.html.

McMillan, D. W., & Chavis, D. M. (1986). A sense of community: A definition and theory. In J. R. Newbrough & D. M. Chavis (eds.), *Journal of Community Psychology, 14*(1), 6–23.

National Education Association. (2015). *Wikipedia.* https://en.wikipedia.org/wiki/National_Education_Association.

National Education Association. Issues and Action. (2015). http://www.nea.org/home/IssuesAndAction.html.

O'Brien, A. (2012, March 21). The importance of community involvement in schools. *Edutopia.* http://www.edutopia.org/blog/community-parent-involvement-essential-anne-obrien.

U.S. Census Bureau. (2012). School districts. https://www.census.gov/did/www/schooldistricts/.

Chapter 8

Intergenerational Influences
The Power of Education on Children's Lives
Bruce S. Cooper

In 1994, the first International Conference on Population and Development was convened. A twenty-year agreement was then established among 179 countries to educate peoples for sustained development and attention to human rights and needs. National policies and action plans continue to be developed to provide resources, more opportunities for mobility, and skill development among all ages, genders, and religious groups to benefit international market productivity and the quality of life. This section summarizes the efforts across the world to offer great opportunities and upward mobility to each and all generations and groups.

What can we learn from research, experience, and personal triumphs of the individuals who have struggled—and succeeded? And how can we educate whole communities to experience success for their children and themselves? A number of possible programs can be used to improve neighborhoods and communities that are underserved or ignored. We explore the possibilities of schooling for parents and their young children in literacy and language development while examining studies that attend to the whole child.

Research indicates the influence and effects of the dysfunctional stress from hunger, familial dysfunction, environmental factors, crime, and pollution on a child's cognitive potential. Entire communities in both urban and rural settings are the most vulnerable, affecting the future opportunities of children. As John U. Ogbu (1974) explained in his book *The Next Generation: An Ethnography of Education in an Urban Neighborhood*, children growing up in low-income families in one California community—where the vast majority (92 percent) in schools were Mexican Americans and blacks—have problems, based on their low income and family influence:

The study reported here probes into the reasons for many children from the neighborhood failing in public schools. The goal was to study how the people in Stockton, including Burghersiders, conceptualize their educational system and their place in it, and how these conceptualizations influence the way they behave within the institution. (Ogbu, 1974, p. 2)

INTERGENERATIONAL INFLUENCE

According to the Organisation for Economic Co-operation and Development (OECD, 2010), "Intergenerational educational persistence partly reflects the influence of family background on cognitive skills developed during secondary education" (p. 184). Educated parents or those understanding the importance of learning for social mobility insist on supporting their children's learning and study. Even without the resources, parents' attitudes and interest have great influence on goals and outcomes for their children. Reading the personal biographies in this book presented in chapter 1, we are all aware, although not admitted by everyone, that the income divide in the United States is an economic fact and has increased over the last two decades.

The demands for a more skilled labor force have grown with the advent of technology. Educational programs have not often kept pace; and, in fact, with the advent of a one-size-fits-all curriculum and standardized testing, have regressed in applicability for real-life employability. The resulting issue is the lack of socioeconomic status (SES) and upward social mobility for many of these stuck in environments with few resources. The perpetuation of low income and less than adequate education are correlated and reinforced.

Research indicates that some countries where the Program for International Student Assessment (PISA) is administered—for example, France, New Zealand, Austria, United Kingdom, and the United States, among others—show the largest discrepancy between socioeconomic status and student performance in secondary education.

This chapter explores five related issues around the wealth and influence of generations of the family in helping the nation's children to prosper. For wealth, good education, quality health care, and well-being appear to be passed from one generation to the next, parents to children, and then to grandchildren. Conversely, adults who are poor, uneducated, in poor health, and not improving have problems supporting and helping their offspring to do better, get a higher quality (often expensive) education, earn more income, be healthier, and live better lives. Sad but true.

The five foci of this chapter are as follows:

1. The relationships between the generations in well-to-do countries like the United States.
2. Practices and methods for improving the next generation.

3. The critical role that schools play in the intergenerational improvement process.
4. The major hindrances to intergenerational growth and what can be done to fix them.
5. The funding and financial level's effects on the intergenerational process, and what has been tried by courts and governments to fix it.

THE FIVE CRITICAL *P*S RELATED TO INTERGENERATIONAL QUALITY AND EFFECTS

The five *P*s in the generational effects on kids are some or all of the following: (1) parents, with the family's political power; (2) family's economic processes for gaining and using resources and influence; (3) children's patience and persistence; (4) available government policies and programs to help children in school and beyond; and (5) to overcome problems with good policies and programs, as discussed below.

1. Parents' (and Grandparents') Actions and Influence with Kids

In Hebrew, "from generation to generation" is *L'Dor Va'dor* and recognizes the importance and influence of one generation on the next ones, as children and even grandchildren grow up, feeling the effects and effectiveness of their families. There is little doubt that one generation has real power and important influence over the next generation, socially, economically, and personally.

As children grow up and their mothers and fathers are often closest to them, parental influence increases. As Carl Pickhardt (2010) explains, "Children observe their parents more closely, appraise their parents more carefully, and know their parents better than parents do the child. How could it be otherwise? The positional power difference makes this inequality necessarily so" (p. 1).

In the "virtual world" adolescents often have access to cars and computers, in different forms, as Pickhardt (2010) further explains:

> I believe the role is basically the same as parenting in the real world. That is, to be kept adequately informed by the adolescent about what is going on so they can discharge their duty adequately to inform the teenager about risks to watch out for, rules to follow, and self-management responsibilities to be learned. (p. 4)

The great "freedom machine" in the real world is the automobile. Being trained and licensed to drive can open one up to physical travel for independence, mobility, and work. And the great "freedom machine" in the virtual world is now the computer. Whatever we consider cars and computers to be, it is parents who are critical in rearing, supporting, and shaping the attitudes and practices of their children, relating to *technology*, a major step in the intergenerational process.

Table 8.1 Average Weekly Childcare Costs for Families with Children Younger Than Age Five and Employed Mothers Who Make Payments

	Average weekly child care costs ($)	Average monthly family income ($)	Percentage of family's income spent on childcare (%)	Mother's average monthly income ($)	Percentage of mother's monthly income spent on child care (%)
All families w/children younger than five	181	8,783	9	3,477	23
All families below the poverty line	103	1,239	36	1,044	43
All families at or above poverty level	188	9,488	9	3,705	22
100–199 percent of poverty level	129	2,751	20	1,667	33
200 plus percent of poverty level	203	11,157	8	4,209	21

Source: US Census Bureau, "Who's minding the kids? Child care arrangements, 2011"; Department of Commerce, 2013.

Grandparents are important, too, although less research has examined children's beliefs, income, and family practices based on their grandparents. For some kids hardly ever (or never) see or come to know their grandparents, who have died, moved away, or remained apart from their grandkids and family for life-death, health, physical, and psychological reasons and conditions. More research should be done on the generational influence of grandma and grandpa (see Denham & Smith, 1989).

2. Process of Economics for Gaining and Using Resources

In the early years, before school starts, many parents who work, and try to earn a decent living for their kids and family, find they need day care and childcare for the family and the economic problems involved (see table 8.1).

Data show middle-class family income rising slowing, minimally while day care costs are rising faster. Thus, we see the rising need for childcare despite ever-higher costs, against the ability of middle-income people to pay for the service. As the Center for American Progress (2014) reports, "To have a strong and growing economy, we need a strong and growing middle class. However, the middle-class share of national income has fallen, wages are stagnant, and the middle-class in the United States are no longer the world's wealthiest."

But income is only one side of the story. The cost of the basic pillars of the middle class—security, childcare, housing, and health care, as well as setting aside modest savings for retirement or college—are rising faster than ever.

In short, the American middle class is in serious trouble (Center for American Progress, 2014, p. 1).

3. Political Power and Persistence

The third of the *P*s, power and persistence, show that families with higher income often also have greater influence and persistence in helping their children to

a. Get a good education, appropriate for their abilities, needs and interests;
b. Remain healthy through good medical care and prevention, that poor kids may not get;
c. Go to college and get further education, or learn a trade and skills necessary to earning a decent living for their family; and
d. Pass along the appropriate attitude and dedication to family and community that help families to improve their living conditions. (Dahl & Lochner, 2012)

The authority and influence of more middle- and upper-class families have a complex effect on their offspring for generations. We know stories of the Roosevelts, for example, where a great-uncle, Theodore, was US president from 1901 to 1909. And his fifth cousin, Franklin Delano Roosevelt (FDR), was the longest-serving president in US history, during a very difficult period in American life. He led the nation through the terrible economic and human conditions during the Great Depression and then World War II. FDR was elected to office in 1933 and served for four terms, until 1945, when he died at the end of World War II.

FDR had suffered from polio (infantile paralysis) starting at age twenty-one and could hardly stand up without assistance from devices like canes, or human beings to whom he clung. Both legs were damaged. "As World War II drew to a close, Franklin D. Roosevelt's health deteriorated, and on April 12, 1945, while at Warm Springs, Georgia, he died of a cerebral hemorrhage" (White House Historical Society, 1971, p. 2).

Both Roosevelts as presidents (Theodore and Franklin) came from wealthy, related families, particularly FDR, whose parents were able to support the young Franklin at Groton Academy, Harvard (earning a bachelor of arts) and Columbia Universities (law degree), and saw them to the highest office in the land, the presidency.

4. Patience and Persistence

Families should have patience and persistence (the fourth *P*) to ensure that their children get what they need at home, church, mosque or synagogue, and

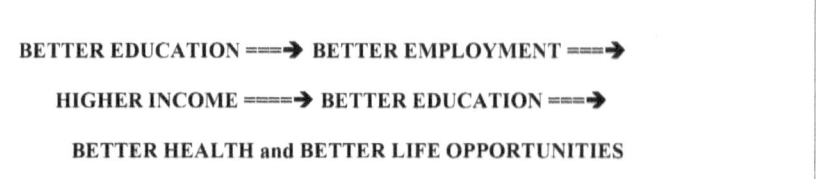

Figure 8.1   Relations of Education to Employment, Income to Education and to Health.

in later life, to encourage their offspring to grow, improve, and prosper. This growth process also takes persistence, as children grow and mature at different rates, and have varying needs, skills, and talents.

We should always consider the complex, dual relationship between family income and good education—and a better life on income and "life-time earning streams." It works both ways, as wealth relates to accessing a good education. And of course, having a better education often means earning higher income through better employment—and health services, and lives (Mulvey & Cooper, 2012). See figure 8.1.

5. Policies and Programs

But families cannot do everything alone. Parents require local community and schools' policies and program resources (the fifth *P*) that enable them to raise their children, to feed and clothe them, and importantly to obtain for every child, no matter what their talents and abilities and needs, *a good education*! Often, families will select a town, neighborhood, community, and school in their residence mainly because of the perceived quality and reputation of local K–12 schools.

But mainly families can buy homes in a community with a good school only if they can afford the housing and related property taxes (which support local public education to large degree); and these resources often affect the overall quality of local schools. Thus, better schools often raise local property values, which means higher property taxes that requires higher incomes to pay the costs. It's to a great degree cyclical, driven by local family income, support including wealth and school costs.

And finally, overcoming problems with effective policies and programs will always pose problems for families and society. Each generation appears to have its own unique qualities and needs; and government leaders and educators should work together to improve education for everyone over time. Already federal, state, and local government leaders (e.g., presidents, governors, mayors, and school administrators) have noted difficulties in intergenerational power, education, and opportunity, and have done much to overcome these problems.

Here are five key steps in school reforms in education policies/programs over the last century or so that have worked to equalize and improve education for more and different children:

Step 1: Combating Racial Segregation and Educational Isolation

First, when families of color, particularly in the South, were "segregated" and often prevented from attending better, middle-class "white" public—and most private—schools, the courts finally intervened, ruling in 1954 and 1955 that school districts could not be segregated by race. In fact, housing and even trains were segregated legally earlier under the *Plessy* (1891) decision that was overturned a half-century later by *Brown v. Board of Education of Topeka, Kansas* (347 U.S. 483), based on the civil rights amendments to the US Constitution that were not effective in desegregating local public schools, as commentators explained:

> Despite these Constitutional Amendments, African Americans were often treated differently than whites in many parts of the country, especially in the South. In fact, many state legislatures enacted laws that led to the legally mandated segregation of the races. In other words, the laws of many states decreed that blacks and whites could not use the same public facilities, ride the same buses, attend the same schools, etc.
>
> These laws came to be known as Jim Crow laws. Although many people felt that these laws were unjust, it was not until the 1890s that they were directly challenged in court. In 1892, an African-American man named Homer Plessy refused to give up his seat to a white man on a train in New Orleans, as he was required to do by Louisiana state law [leading to another desegregation case]. (uscourts.gov, History of Brown v. Board of Education Re-enactment)

However, with the US Supreme Court's *Brown* decisions in 1954 and 1955, schools across the nation began to desegregate; and Black and Latino, and later Asian children were given access to better, more racially diverse schools and better educations. The decisions under *Brown* were actually given different interpretations and outcomes in different states. And as uscourts.gov reports, "The cases that came to be known as *Brown v. Board of Education* (1954, 1955) were actually the name given to five separate cases that were heard by the U.S. Supreme Court concerning the issue of segregation in public schools" (p. 1).

Step 2. Local Property Wealth, Education Resources, and Quality

Next, after the movements against racial discrimination, came the tougher issues of family income and community wealth's effects on education and how this "socioeconomic status" (SES) affected the quality of schools—and the resources available to help the poor and other students get a quality education in public schools. Following President John F. Kennedy's concerns and Lyndon B. Johnson's War on Poverty, many local communities began to sue their state to equalize education funding per-pupil and quality and opportunities, state by state.

The first case was in California in 1975, when the impoverished Serrano family brought a case against the state to equalize funding for schools in poor neighborhoods and school districts. The case was called *Serrano v. Priest*, in which the Serrano family symbolically sued Mary Baker Priest, who had been the US treasurer and later became the California secretary of the treasury. Not her fault; but the state bore responsibility for the low tax funds available for schools in poor neighborhoods and school districts. As the courts determined:

> California's method of funding public education, because of district-to-district disparities, "fails to meet the requirements of the equal protection clause of the Fourteenth Amendment of the United States Constitution and the California Constitution." [As] a direct result of the financing scheme, they are required to pay a higher tax rate than [taxpayers] in many other school districts to obtain for their children the same or lesser educational opportunities afforded children in those other districts. [That] an actual controversy has arisen and now exists between the parties as to the validity and constitutionality of the financing scheme under the Fourteenth Amendment of the United States Constitution and under the California Constitution. (Wikipedia, *Serrano v. Priest*)

The California Supreme Court agreed with the plaintiffs, largely based on equal-protection arguments, and returned the *Serrano v. Priest* case to the trial court for further proceedings. In summary:

> A decade after the Civil Rights Act and the Elementary and Secondary Education Act and two decades after the Supreme Court's decision in *Brown v. Board of Education*, the meaning of the phrase *equal educational opportunity* still was not entirely clear. What *was* clear, however, was the rapidly growing *cost* of public schools throughout the nation. Despite the infusion of federal aid that had followed the Education Amendments of 1974, local districts struggled to find the resources needed to meet the demand for specialized educational services. (SIFEPP, nd.)

Since the *Serrano* decision in the 1970s in California, many other states have had similar cases, and have worked to equalize spending on schools across districts, per-pupil, more equitably, usually by setting maximum funding levels or giving more state aid to poor local school districts. The limited uses of the US Constitution to protect the rights of families to equal funding of schools in Texas came with *San Antonio Independent School District v. Rodriguez* (1973). The question posed to the Supreme Court was

> Did Texas' public education finance system violate the Fourteenth Amendment's Equal Protection Clause by failing to distribute funding equally among its school districts?
>
> No. The Court refused to examine the system with strict scrutiny since there is no fundamental right to education in the Constitution and since the system did not systematically discriminate against all poor people in Texas. Given the similarities between Texas' system and those in other states, it was clear to the Court that the funding scheme was not "so irrational as to be invidiously discriminatory." Justice Powell argued that on the question of wealth and education, "the Equal Protection Clause does not require absolute equality or precisely equal advantages." ("San Antonio Independent School District v. Rodriguez," p. np)

Education remains primarily a state-by-state matter, as family income, property wealth, and local property taxes for education support vary by state, community (neighborhood), and school.

Step 3: Generational Help and Education for Children with "Special Needs"

The next step in the US effort was to provide all children with a quality educational opportunity, including those intellectually, physically, and emotionally limited and "disabled" children in public schools. About 12 percent of children have some intellectual limitations, which the schools were poorly equipped to handle and fix. Thus, the Education for All Handicapped Children Act—sometimes referred to using the acronyms EAHCA or EHA, or Public Law 94–142 (PL 94–142)—was enacted by the US Congress in 1975.

While "ability grouping" was common, the least able were nationally ignored and inadequately served. Children on crutches and in wheelchairs often found schools difficult if not impossible to enter, with stairs and landings; less able, "retarded" students found schools too difficult; "emotionally disturbed" children were punished and isolated for interrupting classes and upsetting teachers and fellow students.

Again, while the wealthier families could often fund a private and/or religious program or school to educate their children who were blind, deaf, physically disabled, or "emotionally disturbed," parents with fewer resources simply had no school, or limited education, available for their children. Traditional disabilities (blind, deaf, and immobilized) had long been recognized, while less able, "mentally retarded," and "emotionally disturbed" poor children had little generational help.

Examining deafness as a disability for students of school age, Martha Barnun (1984) has written about this group of students, even when occurring among bi-language students. She found that

> Due to the inherent differences in oral-aural and visual-manual languages, particularly the mediums through which they are learned, the overwhelming majority of deaf children can neither learn English effectively through speech-reading and written English, nor can they receive their education through speech-reading, written English, or manual forms of English and achieve anything even nearly comparable to the achievements of their hearing peers. Research is consistently showing that native signers do better academically and maintain that advantage throughout their school years. Instruction through a natural sign language is also a benefit, and the transition to teaching through English can be successfully accomplished at about the fifth-grade level. (Barnum, 1984, p. 404)

Intergenerational knowledge and influence are probably most noteworthy and needed for kids with any disability—physically, emotionally, and/or intellectually. Hence, the power of these parental generations upon the education and opportunities are most noteworthy and critical for the approximately 4.5 million children with some limitations or disabilities.

As Kemp et al. (2016) explains: "All children need love, encouragement, and support, and for kids with learning disabilities, such positive reinforcement can help ensure that they emerge with a strong sense of self-worth, confidence, and the determination to keep going even when things are tough" (p. np). Kemp and her colleagues further suggest the following tactics for dealing with schools on behalf of these children:

Tips for Communicating with Your Child's School:
Being a vocal advocate for a child can be challenging. You'll need superior communication and negotiation skills, and the confidence to defend your child's right to a proper education.

- *Clarify your goals.* Before meetings, write down what you want to accomplish. Decide what is most important, and what you are willing to negotiate.
- *Be a good listener.* Allow school officials to explain their opinions. If you don't understand what someone is saying, ask for clarification. "What I hear you saying is . . ." can help ensure that both parties understand.
- *Offer new solutions.* You have the advantage of not being a "part of the system," and may have new ideas. Do your research and find examples of what other schools have done.
- *Keep the focus.* The school system is dealing with a large number of children; you are only concerned with your child. Help the meeting stay focused on

your child. Mention your child's name frequently, don't drift into generalizations, and resist the urge to fight larger battles.
- *Stay calm, collected and positive.* Go into the meeting assuming that everyone wants to help. If you say something you regret, simply apologize and try to get back on track.
- *Don't give up easily.* If you're not satisfied with the school's response, try again. (Kemp et al., 2016, p. np)

GENERATIONS MATTER: NEW GENERATIONS, NEW NEEDS, NEW SOLUTIONS

It now appears that the next generation of children—who are struggling in school and beyond—are often "foreign born" or whose parents were not born in the United States. In fact, statistics show that that many children born in the United States have at least one parent born in another country. As Cruz (2009) explained:

> At the current pace, by the year 2040, one in three children will grow up in a household with at least one foreign-born parent (Suarez-Orozco et al., 2008). Due to growing disparities in educational achievement among first, second and third generation students, scholars have attempted to explain the success of those first and second-generation immigrant students who excel. Pereira et al. (2011) found that first generation immigrant students are more likely to drop out of high school (at a rate of 13 percent) than their U.S.-born peers with foreign-born parents. . . . In particular, I challenge immigrant optimism-defeatist theories as potential explanations of the differences between first, second, and third generation immigrant youth's educational attainment. (p. np)

As we examine the power and limitations of parents, grandparents, and other family members on children's education, we see evidence of the *power of generations.* As we discussed in this chapter, children are often affected and limited by what their parents and communities bring to the education situation. The United States has absorbed, taught, and found employment for millions of foreign-born people from across the world.

Thus, governments and public charities now try to overcome these generational limitations by lobbying for greater public support, more attention from educators *and* politicians, and everyone for all generations rising to the challenge (Duncan & Murnane, 2014). As Nancy Folbre from the *New York Times* (2014) recently reported:

> Allowing students some voice in their enrollment decisions, and fostering the stability and commitment of the teaching staff, has created a more sustainable

social environment, which, in turn, has increased the graduation rates of low-income students by seven-percentage points. (p. np)

Our kids and society depend on education—for us all. And we want to make our families proud, from generation to generation, and reward them for their work and sacrifices for children to get a good productive education, from generation to generation—as expressed in Hebrew: *L'Dor Va'dor.*

REFERENCES

Barnum, M. (1984). In support of bilingual/bicultural education for deaf children. *American Annals of the Deaf, 129*(5), 404–408.
Center for American Progress. (2014, September 24). *The middle class squeeze.* http://app.mx3.americanprogressaction.org.
Cooper, B. S., & Mulvey, J. D. (2012). *Intersections of children's health, education, and welfare.* New York: Palgrave Macmillan.
Cruz, V. (2009). Educational attainment of first and second generation immigrant youth. *Research Brief no. 5.* Washington, DC: Urban Institute, Summer Academy for Public Policy Analysis and Research.
Dahl, G. B., & Lochner, L. (2012). The impact of family income on child achievement: Evidence from the earned. *American Economic Review* 2012, *102*(5): 1927–1956.
Denham, T. E., & Smith, C. W. (1989, July). The influence of grandparents on grandchildren: A review of the literature and resources. *Family Relations, 38*(3), 345–350.
Duncan, G. G., & Murnane, R. J. (2014). *Restoring opportunity: The crisis of inequality and the challenge for American education.* New York: Sage Foundation and Harvard University Press.
Folbre, N. (2014). Helping low-income children succeed. *New York Times.* economix.blogs.nytimes.com/2014/03/24/a-fair-chance-for-children/?_r=0.
Kemp, G., Smith, M., & Segal, J. (last updated May 2016). Helping children with learning disabilities: Practical parenting tips for home and school. HelpGuide. www.helpguide.org/articles/learning-disabilities/helping-children-with-learning-disabilities.htm.
OECD. (2010). A family affair: Intergenerational social mobility across OECD countries. In *Economic Policy Reforms: Going for Growth.* Paris: OECD Publishing. doi:10.1787/growth-2010-en.
OECD. (2011). *Lessons from PISA for the United States: Strong performers and successful reformers in education.* Paris: OECD Publishing. doi:10.1787/9789264096660-en.
Ogbu, J. U. (1974). *The next generation: An ethnography of education in an urban neighborhood.* New York: Academic Press.
Perreira, K. M., Harris, K. M., & Lee, D. (2011). Immigrant youth in the labor market. *Work and Occupations, 34*(1): 5–34.

Pickhardt, C. (2010, October 18). Surviving (your child's) adolescence: Welcome to the hard half of parenting. *Psychology Today*, 5–11.

Potochnick, S., R., & Perreira, K. M. (2010). Depression and anxiety among first-generation immigrant Latino youth: Key correlates and implications for future research. *The Journal of Nervous and Mental Disease*, *198*(7): 470–477.

San Antonio Independent School District v. Rodriguez. (n.d.). *Oyez*. https://www.oyez.org/cases/1972/71-1332.

SIFEPP (nd). States' Impact on Federal Education Policy Project. New York State Archives. http://www.archives.nysed.gov/research/edpolicy/home.

Wikipedia. (last modified April 22, 2016). *Serrano v. Priest*. https://en.wikipedia.org/wiki/Serrano_v._Priest.

Chapter 9

Summary and Future Implications

Janet D. Mulvey and Bruce S. Cooper

The end of the twentieth and beginning of the twenty-first centuries have seen the moving of families from isolation to connection through technological advances in the communication media, sharing of ideas, and seeking help online. The opportunities to develop and sustain broad regional, national, and even international communities through education have never been greater.

And education is now moving in the same direction—from local to regional to national—and also international. The power of education has never been greater; and harnessing this force and process is critical to any and all societies.

We are witnessing how easy access to information is changing perspectives for human rights and knowledge worldwide—and how we are learning more about cultures very different from our own. Internalizing this knowledge should help us understand the needs in our own impoverished areas, in inner cities and rural areas. Quality education for all peoples, regardless of their political influence, is a right that should and must be honored everywhere if the world is to improve for all, regardless of their locations, ethnicities, and resources (wealth and income).

This chapter will summarize the research on needs and evidence of the real power of education for those who have and continue to struggle economically, medically, socially—and educationally.

WHAT'S OUR FUTURE?

We have seen the power of education through the stories of those who have overcome the fates of their peers, nations, and communities. "Knowledge is power" is not just a cliché but also a fact witnessed here in the United States and abroad.

The economic differences between the 1 and 99 percent brought to light during the Occupation of Wall Street movement have not diminished. Poverty and being deprived of education, medical care, and social support continue to reinforce the struggles for equal opportunity for all in living conditions across the nation.

Education to prepare our youth to meet the challenges of the twenty-first century is paramount to our society in America and worldwide. This chapter provides suggestions for educating individuals, neighborhoods, and communities to improve the overall quality of life, sustain our democracy, and keep us strong in the international marketplace.

We think that good, high-performing students, and future quality teachers are so vital to better education and to life, growth, jobs, and families, who need to know how to earn a living and contribute to their communities and their schools. We must somehow bring education together with the lives and accomplishments of some interesting, outstanding people. And kids being healthy usually means that children can attend school regularly and participate in classes and feel up to learning. And once one is well educated, one can learn and know about a "healthy lifestyle" and what preventative and appropriate treatments can lead to a better life, better employment, and higher incomes.

Thus, this book has incorporated both the personal and technical dimensions of the powers of education, and should help families, communities, educational institutions, and governments to move toward helping everyone get an education, to the benefit of all.

This final chapter reviews our findings and posits steps that societies and communities (and families) can and must take to break the terrible relationship between family's income (wealth), education (both received for parents and available for their children), and the ways that a poor education, poor income, poor wealth, and poor health care and treatments interrelate and must be somehow improved: working from generation to family to child to adult to offspring—and on and on.

We suggest breaking the negative relationships and starting to provide more children a decent quality education, better jobs and careers, greater income, more quality health care, and expanded educational opportunities for their children, and even their grandchildren. We have already shown the power of education in life, learning, careers, income, health, and thus, for the quality of life. Let's take a few cases as examples.

HOW CAN WE ASSURE A GOOD EDUCATION FOR ALL CHILDREN?

When comparing the United States with other nations, one big set of differences is the universality of public, free, and available education for all.

The United States has a long tradition of free, local public education, while other nations have greater varieties of schools and more limited access for some groups.

When we compare education and health in the United Kingdom with the United States, for example, we see that UK has universal health care, but a range of quite expensive private schools that are exclusive and elite. If a child in the UK (England, Wales, or Scotland) is sick, the state health care system is available without charge—what is often called "socialized medicine."

So wealth and medical care are less associated; while in United States, when getting sick and being poor, children may end up the emergency room or clinic. Poverty and illness are closely associated; and poor children are more likely to die in their first year on Earth than infants from wealthier families who can afford better prenatal care, private infant delivery, and childcare from birth.

HEALTH AND WEALTH: HOW TRYING TO STAY WELL—AND ALIVE—ARE COSTLY

Thus, health and wealth are closely correlated, as the United States has less free, available, quality medical care for the poor and needy than many other countries. As Levy and Sidel (2013) explain,

> We live in the richest nation on earth. Yet 15% of the U.S. population (about 46 million people) lives below the poverty line—earning about $23,000 for a family of four. Almost 25% of children live in poverty. The number of American households living on $2 or less grew by 130% between 1996 and 2011. Actual household median income decreased by more than 8% between 2007 and 2012. And the number of homeless children in preschools and schools recently rose 10% within one year.
>
> If you are poor, you are more likely to develop many illnesses, more likely to become injured, more likely to become disabled, and more likely to die early. You are less likely to have access to high-quality medical care—or any medical care at all—and less likely to have access to preventive services. (p. np)

Pollack et al. (2014), in *The Journal of Preventative Medicine,* describes the role of medical help in not only treating disease but also in actually preventing it. The relationship is complex, and relates to family's education, income, and health care. See figure 9.1.

Health research rarely measures and applies the patients' accumulated *wealth* or *income* to reflect socioeconomic status/position (SES) and its effects on health and medical care and general well-being. To determine whether health research should more frequently include measures of wealth, this section begins to assess the relationship between *wealth* and *health.*

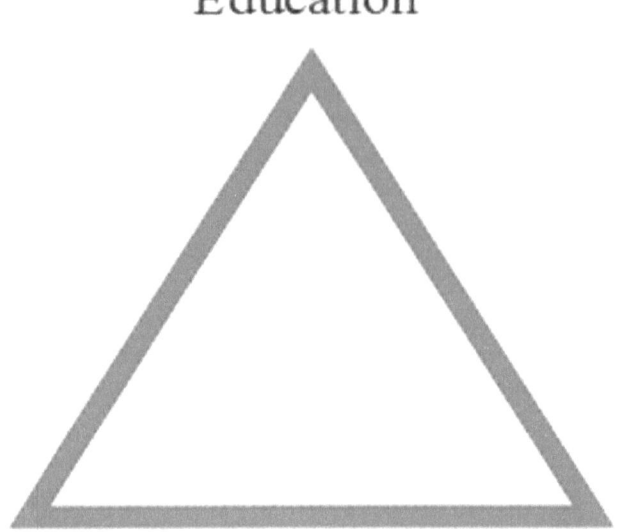

Figure 9.1 Relationship between Education, Health, and Income. *Source*: Graph created from Deaton (2003).

Studies published from 1990 to 2006 were systematically reviewed. These studies used wealth—and at least one other SES measure as predictor variables, and health-related outcomes as key dependent variables.

Results

Twenty-nine studies met our inclusion criteria. Measures of wealth varied greatly. In most research, *greater wealth was associated with better health*, even after adjusting for other personal variables. These findings appeared most consistent when using detailed wealth measures including specific income, assets, and debts, rather than a single income variable.

Adjusting for wealth generally decreased observed racial/ethnic disparities in health. When we put "health," "education," and "income" (welfare) into a "relational triangle" (figure 9.1), we see the complex but important relationships that shape children for generations.

We find that *employment* is a key factor, as most employment usually includes a health care plan and provision as part of the job benefits package. As Ron Shinkman (2015) quotes ConnectedHealth:

"The connection between health and financial stress has long been studied, and employers are increasingly recognizing that concerns about health and financial security make their way into the workplace in the form of decreased productivity, higher absenteeism, and less 'presenteeism,'" according to a white paper published by ConnectedHealth. (p. 4)

And not only is health care expensive and not always available to the poor, but it is sometimes ineffective if patients cannot afford related diagnoses and treatments that follow up on initial examinations and tests.

As we showed in this book and our earlier one (Mulvey & Cooper, 2012), data indicate that many families build up "health-related debt" when trying to pay for the high costs of medical treatments and assistance. And, in fact, "Medical debt is by far the leading cause of bankruptcy in the United States" (Shinkman, 2015, p. 2).

Here's a report on the costs and problems of paying for health care in the United States:

"The Consumer Financial Protection Bureau reported last year that 43 million Americans have *medical debts* that they have yet to pay; and more than half of the debts that get referred to collection agencies are medical in nature" (Shinkman, 2015, p. 3). Thus, not only is health care often unavailable to many poor families;, but also, trying to pay the bills related to health care themselves can be expensive and financially destructive, with more than 22 million Americans going bankrupt each year in their efforts to find, receive, and pay for health care. The American Health Information Management Association (AHIMA) likewise reports that more than half the Americans who declare bankruptcy are in debt from medical costs.

ConnectedHealth's Jo Donlan (2005) states that "since more than 60 percent of bankruptcies in the United States are caused by medical bills, it's important that employees understand the connection between *health and wealth*." Donlan further explains that

> We have brought together experts in healthcare, benefits, insurance, technology and design to help make benefits easier for employers. Our goal is to ensure that their employees achieve better health and financial security. Since 2009, ConnectedHealth's seasoned team has helped hundreds of businesses nationwide re-imagine the way they deliver customized benefit to their entire workforce. (http://www.connectedhealth/com/about-us/)

Thus, the relationships between health and income go both ways: a good job, and thus better income, often makes better medical care affordable and available for families, which benefits their kids. Being a healthy child can often mean better school attendance, concentration on schoolwork, and a happier time at school, home, and in the community. As the National Research Council and the Institute of Medicine (2004) explain,

> It is in the national interest to have healthy children. Healthy children are more ready and able to learn and, in the longer term, are more likely to become healthy adults who will contribute as a productive citizenry and workforce to the continued vitality of society. . . . To ensure healthy children and create a healthy nation, meaningful information must be collected to support a broader conceptualization of health; this information must be used by federal, state, and local decision makers to inform interventions, programs, and policies. (2004, p. 11)

Conversely, unemployment or a low-level, poorly paying (often temporary) job usually means little or no health care funding or provision, as the research has shown.

IMPLICATIONS

Health care studies should include family wealth, employment, and income as important SES indicators. Failure to measure wealth may often result in underestimating the contribution of socioeconomic standing to health, such as when studying the etiology of racial/ethnic disparities. Validation is needed for simpler approaches to measuring wealth that would be feasible and useful in health care studies.

Even the death rates relate to education, as shown in figure 9.2 below, for rates of men (gray) and women (orange by education levels below): we see that less education means higher levels of death, earlier with 665.2 men per thousand, and 387.4 women per thousand die before reaching 65 years of age. In comparison, the rate for the same age group who had some college experience or a college is 156.8 for those women. Amazing. It is hard to tell whether it's the education level or family income that accounts for the longer life. But either way, being educated can mean higher income and lower death rates! (See figure 9.2.)

What is the relationship between higher income and a good education? Does more spending increase students' learning? And how can we improve schooling to raise standards of living? We have already analyzed and discussed the income–education connection in great detail in this book. Having a good job (and occupation), usually based on a quality education, often means higher income (and better health care coverage and educational opportunities for oneself and one's offspring).

Thus, this money often grants three key advantages for families: (1) to live well, (2) to provide better medical care, and (3) to give their children access to

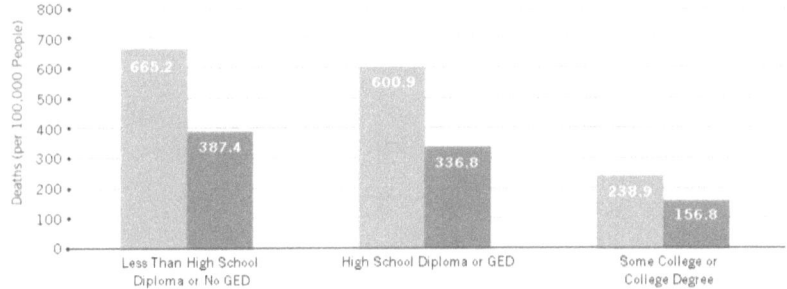

Figure 9.2 Mortality Rates for People Ages Twenty-Five to Sixty-Four, by Sex and Level of Education, 2007 (gray bars are men; black, women). *Source*: National Vital Statistics Report, 2007.

a better, quality education. We examined how higher income enables families to purchase (or rent) a home in a better neighborhood or town with higher quality schools.

In fact, during the last forty years or so, since the two *Serrano v. Priest* decisions in California in 1971 and again in 1975, the state courts have recognized the inequalities among school districts, based mainly on differences in local property values, which are usually the main source of local taxes and educational income, as summarized and supported in the California decision in *Serrano II* in 1976:

> In *Serrano v. Priest* (1976) 18 Cal.3d 728 [135 Cal. Rptr. 345, 557 P.2d 929] (hereafter cited as *Serrano II*), we affirmed a judgment of the Los Angeles County Superior Court, entered on September 3, 1974, which held essentially (1) that the then-existing California public school financing system was invalid as in violation of state *constitutional* provisions guaranteeing *equal protection of the laws*; and (2) that the said system must be brought into constitutional compliance within a period of six years from the date of entry of judgment, the trial court retaining jurisdiction for the purpose of granting any necessary future relief. That judgment is now final.

One other major research project (Card & Payne, 2002) explored the effects of a state court's attempt that failed to equalize local school spending. Card and Payne thus explained:

> We find that in the aftermath of a negative court decision, states tend to increase the relative funding available to lower-income districts. The second question is whether shifts in the amount of funding available from state sources leads to any change in the relative spending of richer and poorer districts. (p. 80)

Thus, attempts to equalize spending, by going to court, may tip the balance toward greater equity, since state governors and legislatures get the message and change their policies. We know that equalizing income and property values across the various school districts may not be easily accomplished; in addition, we cannot determine the exact effects of higher spending on teaching and learning in the classroom.

1. Education and Income

We then looked at how more, better, and higher education affected individuals' jobs and income. Again, it seems clear that having high school and college degrees improves job opportunities and income, although we see that different jobs, even with a college degree (BA), can mean different levels of income—as we compare a variety of positions and jobs. As Hoffmann and Jensen (2013) report, "The main finding . . . is that the canonical correlation analysis showed a result that could be interpreted as a substantive relationship between status, income and education" (p. 14).

Other routes in education may lead to a choice of profession that is lower paying but more satisfying to the individual. Either way, whether to gain education for greater wealth or greater satisfaction, the key is the possibility to choose.

So, it's quite clear: the relationship between education and income works both ways. That is, the more income, the better education the children can obtain; and better education, once gained in high school and college and other graduate and professional degrees, the better jobs and higher income. Better income means better education, and better education often leads to better employment and higher, more consistent income. Income leads to education, and education helps with better employment. Back and forth!

2. Education and Health

The final relationship also seems clear: as folks get educated, regardless of income, they are more able to live better lives, eat better foods, take fewer drugs, and thus enjoy healthier lives. Research confirms that better education often means better health (Hitti, 2009). And the report shows that education makes a difference when it comes to health: "'Education is a marker for an array of opportunities and resources that can lead people to better or worse health,' David R. Williams, PhD, the commission's staff director, said in a news conference."

For instance, Williams explains that a "poor education can lead to limited job options, lower incomes, and greater work-related stress. Down the road, that can limit a family's chances to live in a healthy home and neighborhood, increasing their exposure to harmful conditions and further emotional stresses that can lead to illness." (Hitti, 2009)

David R. Williams, an African American medical researcher, has done much to connect health to race and racism, and SES with health. As one description by the Harvard School of Public Health explains:

> He is internationally recognized as a leading social scientist focused on social influences on health. His research has enhanced our understanding of the complex ways in which race, racism, socioeconomic status, stress, health behaviors and religious involvement can affect physical and mental health.

Research also shows that education and health work both ways: if one is healthier as a young person, one can attend school regularly and be more alert and energetic, paying closer attention in classes and labs. And if one is well educated, presumably individuals can "self-diagnose" themselves and know what to do: see a doctor, change diet, get more exercise, sleep longer and better, take vitamins, and so forth. As Hernandez-Murillo and Martinek (2011) explain,

> For health and education both reinforce one another: being healthy means taking on the schooling and world; self-regulating foods, drugs, and other personal actions. *The more you learn, the more you earn!* This phrase has been used by education proponents to encourage young students to stay in school or pursue higher education. But higher lifetime earnings are not the only positive outcome from increased schooling.
>
> As it turns out, the more you learn, the more you live in good health. For example, in 2007, the age-adjusted mortality rate (measured in deaths per 100,000 people) among American males between 25 and 64 years was 665.2 for individuals without a high school diploma, 600.9 for individuals who completed high school and 238.9 for individuals with some college or higher. (1) In terms of healthy behaviors, the estimated incidence of smoking among American males over the age of 25 with a bachelor's degree or higher was 10.4 percent, while this figure among males with a high school degree or less was about 30 percent. (2) Similar differences exist for obesity and for alcohol use.
>
> If more education can lead to better health, addressing the processes by which differences in education translate into differences in health can be useful to

public policymakers. Identifying a causal relationship is of crucial importance in the design. For example, if more education *causes* better health, then policies to increase education might also be effective at improving health in the population. However, if the association (often called correlation) between education and health exists because better health allows individuals to attain a better education (reverse causation) or because the correlation between education and health results from the *correlation* of education with other factors that also improve health (such as income of the parents), then education-improving policies might not be effective at improving health.

Better education not only improves the chances of better health, but it also seems to increase one's health and life span.

Note: Data are for 22 reporting states and the District of Columbia that use the 2003 version of the U.S. Standard Certificate of Death. Data for states that use the 1989 version of the U.S. Standard Certificate of Death, which classifies educational attainment by years of schooling instead of level, exhibit the same trend. (Hernandez-Murill & Martinek, 2011)

NEXT STEPS

National educational research studies are clear. We, as a nation, must use data connected to demographical change, both culturally and socioeconomically, to correct the trajectory for educational proficiency. The public school system once created as a means to educate the populace has been permitted to decline in favor of more selective and private education afforded by the more affluent.

In 1953 the *New York Times* reported that "Horace Mann believed that the success of the country depended on 'intelligence and virtue in the masses of the people'—'if we do not prepare our children to be good citizens—then our republic must go down to destruction'" (p. np). Mann's influence created the Normal School, now the public school, to guarantee free education for all of the nation's children.

According to the 2012 Voter Turnout Report, approximately ninety-three million eligible voters did not vote, the percentage dropped from 62.3 percent in 2008 to 57.5 percent in 2012. Education is key in impressing the significance of selecting a government representative of all cultures and values, ideals and needs in our diverse population. Without the ability or motivation to listen to political agendas, reflect on their influence for the populace, the control of the country will be affected by fewer than the majority.

Currently, political agendas, policy decisions, and a Supreme Court ruling have permitted segregation by race and socioeconomic status to prevail as the access to public education. Federal and state funding has been distributed unequally among public school districts. Those with more, get more, and those with less, get less.

FUNDING

Inequity in funding for poorer schools has been an issue for decades. As recently as March 12, 2015, the *Washington Post* reports, according to federal data collected in 2012, "in 23 states, state and local governments are together spending less per pupil in the poorest than they are in the most affluent school districts" (p. np). On average the United States spends 15.6 percent fewer dollars on their poor children versus their more affluent.

The lack of equity is a continual problem exacerbating the achievement gap among the poor children in the country. The generational impact is profound. Singer and Pezone (2003) summarize,

> The first step in improving education and the problems plaguing our schools are rooted in the way our society is organize. . . . Businesses and individuals continually seek advantage and higher profits and people on the bottom rung of the economic ladders are stigmatized as failures and blamed for their condition. (p. 145)

Poor education results in producing large segments of society ill prepared to meet the challenges necessary for economic or social mobility, in fact, subjugating them to a much lower standard of living. The daily struggle to meet the necessities for survival leaves little time to support or afford the education of their children. Stress factors, poor access to preventative health care, poor nutrition result in readiness gaps for schooling from its onset throughout.

It is important to note that funding shouldn't be just pouring more money into materials and school supplies: computers, textbooks, salaries, and so on. Funding must incorporate improving the entire community. In Russakoff's book *The Prize* (2015), an accounting of the flawed planning and implementation of $200,000,000 for education in Newark, New Jersey, provides evidence of how political interference, special interests, and infighting took precedence over the needs of impoverished schools and children. Russakoff describes Newark, New Jersey:

> Increasing economic and racial segregation—95% black and Latino, 95% of children in school receive free or reduced lunch prices, 44% live below the

poverty line, 70% are born to unwed mothers and 40% of newborns received little or no prenatal care. . . . These children were disadvantaged before they drew their first breaths. (p. 5)

Funding must target not just the schools but entire communities: health care, environmental cleanup, job training, birth control, and very early prenatal and childcare.

COGNITIVE DEVELOPMENT

Prenatal care and developmental years from birth to age five are the most crucial for cognitive development. Environmental toxins, poor nutrition, stress factors, and lack of intellectual stimulation are the elements dooming children for educational, economic, and social mobility opportunity failure.

Neurological research has connected lack of brain development in the white and gray matter for children living in impoverished environments. Language acquisition, a fundamental for school success, is far below the standard and in fact is one of the main reasons for the inability to comprehend educational terminology and direction.

Consequences for ignoring the proven outcomes in education, social, economic, and physiological development are subjecting large segments of our population to lives that cannot contribute to the overall health and prosperity of our democratic ideals. According to the 2014 Census Bureau, 14.8 percent or 46.7 million people live in poverty in the United States. Politicians and policy makers must look to research and blame themselves, not the people living at or below the poverty line. Understanding and acknowledging the cause and effect of poverty can mobilize federal, state, and local policy makers to address the problem.

POWER FOR SUCCESS

The power of education for success physically, emotionally, and economically can be found in stories affecting those who were able to overcome their poor environments. Each success is connected to the support and education they received within their community.

Antonio Maranganbassa, a Mozambique-born citizen, was abducted to serve as a child soldier in the 1964 Mozambique independence war against Portugal. Never to see his family again, Antonio served with the guerilla forces until rescued in 1972. The rescue by government forces placed Antonio in school, cared for his physical and emotional needs, and provided a quality education. Mr. Maranganbassa today is a successful safari company owner who uses the income from his company to support a school in rural Kitale Kenya. The school built and supported by Mr. Marangabassa is a tribute to his passion for children's education (interview by Mulvey, 2013–15).

Sonia Sotomayor, Supreme Court Justice, began her life in a Bronx housing project. The "American Dream" came to fruition for Justice Sotomayor through her mother's insistence of becoming educated and the support of her extended family. Sotomayor understands the plight of poverty and supports legislation for affirmative action. She writes that affirmative action rightly served "to create the conditions whereby students from disadvantaged backgrounds could be brought to the starting line of a race many were unaware was even being run" (2013, p. 191).

Richard Sherman of football fame comes from a family who struggled with gang and mob violence. His father was shot twice and his friends joined gangs, but Richard took a different path through his athletic acumen and education. Supported in school and active in football, Mr. Sherman graduated high school with honors and attended Stanford University. His experience with racial and ethnic slurs has increased his determination to return to Compton, California, and invest time and money helping disadvantaged youth experience possibilities for success.

Others have become successful in their lives despite early beginnings. What was different? How did they cope? The common denominator for each was their opportunity for an education, regardless of their poor environments. Family and educational support created an opportunity to overcome the surrounding environment and to succeed academically, economically, and socially.

IMPROVING EDUCATION FOR THE MASSES

The successes of a few offer some glimmer of hope for the millions of children who are languishing in poverty with little opportunity for social improvement. Education for communities, funding for resources, and programs implemented through researched practices are the foundation upon which we should build.

The most successful countries in the world have educational standards that professionalize teachers and educational leaders. They are paid fairly and equally regardless of the location of the school. Colleges and universities require prospective teacher registrants to have successfully completed secondary education and be highly qualified for education certification. The United States, in comparison, holds teaching in low regard, attracts the bottom third of ranked candidates, and pays them poorly and unequally.

International schools have consistent standards but also provide consistent quality. In 2015 the top twenty countries in education did not include the United States. What can we learn from the highly diverse acclaimed ranking? Culturally and ethnically different, the top countries share a philosophy about the importance of education to the welfare of the country. Reporting on the traits of success, D. Thani (2015) in MBC Times cites, "Teaching is held in high regard as a career and brings elevated social status" (p. np). Emphasized is the importance of education to the ranked countries. Culturally, all peoples recognize education as one of the most important aspects in life, "education is prized and parents, teachers, and even students care about the results" (p. np).

To break our cycle of failing schools, we need to begin with the children. Families who have generational failure from poor schooling have a difficult time understanding the value and importance of an education.

Early childhood education for those less fortunate is provided and educational and vocational training for parents assists in supporting their children academically and economically. Free health care is provided for all citizens regardless of their ability to pay. Preventative health services for children and emotional counseling for the child and his or her family may alleviate that which Knee (2015) describes: "Too many of Newark's children have suffered unspeakable trauma from their exposure to a combination of violent crime, family turmoil, and deep poverty" (p. 2). It is time for America to put politics aside and represent *all* the people, especially the children.

As this book has shown, health, education, and welfare (income) (HEW) are all strongly interrelated in society. And the federal government, in its own limited way, has tried to improve education, and health, for the greater welfare of all. With the help and support of the Catholic Church in 1965, for example, the US Congress passed the Elementary and Secondary Education Act (ESEA), and finally allowed federal funds to help poor children in public and also private religious schools.

Monsignor Frederick G. Hochwalt worked with President Lyndon B. Johnson, Democrat, to pass ESEA as the first major national effort to help schools, both public and private, to assist poor children get a better education. This federal law followed the desegregation cases in the courts, and efforts to help poor and children of color after the *Brown* decision in 1954 worked to desegregate American schools. And in 1975, many states were expected, following the *Serrano* decision in California and similar decisions in other states, to increase state funding to impoverished local district with large percentages of poor children.

We now have critical, practical suggestions for improving life and using health, education, and income to help all. We make these practical suggestions:

1. Make family health care provision universal for all. The United States truly needs a national health care law and system that gives every family and child free and quality access to needed medical care and treatments (Landry et al., 2000). Most other modern nations have "socialized medicine," or at least universal health care. The United States cannot lag behind forever (see Werner, Maxwell, & Thurber, 2011).

2. Expand quality and practical education for all. Second, since education needs to connect to work and life earnings, we suggest that high school students be taught a skill—and even a trade—to make them more able and employable. Why not introduce concepts of engineering into mathematics and science classes? Both practical and theoretical skills would be improved. Students can thus connect physics, biology, and chemistry to real life (and living) ideas, which would help to learn theory and practice—and to make themselves more employable and potentially healthier, based on their learning.

Much research has shown the complex relationship between life style, income, and health. As O'Neill and Ensle (2014) found in their *Small Steps to Health and Wealth*:

> Many Americans have *both* health and personal finance "issues" in their lives. For example, they may be both overweight *and* overextended on credit card accounts. Yet, until recently, health and personal finances were generally treated as separate topic areas in educational programs, publications, and research (Vitt et al. 2002). 2014 marks the tenth anniversary of Cooperative Extension's *Small Steps to Health and Wealth*™ (SSHW) program.
>
> Conceived at Rutgers University in 2004 to integrate health and personal finance education within a research-based behavioral framework, SSHW is now a signature NIFA-USDA national initiative that has been replicated in more than a dozen states. SSHW encourages people to make positive behavior changes to simultaneously improve their health and personal finances and focuses on small daily action steps that can achieve significant results over time.

3. Improve the economics and income across the nation. We know that poor families need help, to prevent starvation and desperation. Once students are in quality, appropriate schools, where they should be helped to learn their subjects—and applications—the nation may see more and better employment, more and higher levels of income, greater available, quality health care, and a better life for more of its citizens. For as the Social Science Research Council (2015) so aptly explains,

> The most valuable capability people possess is to be alive. Advancing human development requires, first and foremost, expanding the real opportunities

people have to avoid premature death by disease or injury, to enjoy protection from arbitrary denial of life, to live in a healthy environment, to maintain a healthy lifestyle, to receive quality education, medical care, and to attain the highest possible standard of physical and mental health.

The importance of and accessibility to an education has been part of our history even before the Constitution. And while we have struggled to provide schooling for all, we continue to strive for equality and opportunity for all. Democracy that represents all of its people must come to the fore, and as cited in the Northwest Ordinance of 1787, knowledge, "being necessary to good government and the happiness of mankind, schools and the means of education shall forever be encouraged."

REFERENCES

Abecedarian Project. (1972). http://abc.fpg.unc.edu/.
Bowles, S., & Gintis, H. (1976). *Schooling in capitalistic America: Educational reform and the contradictions of economic life*. New York: Basic Books.
Card, D., & Payne, A. A. (2002). School finance reform, the distribution of school spending, and the distribution of student test scores. *Journal of Public Economics*, 83, 49–82.
Deaton, A. (2003). Health, income and equality. National Bureau of Economic Research. http://www.nber.org/reporter/spring03/health.html.
Dewey, J. (1907). *The school and society*. Chicago: University of Chicago Press.
Dickson, M. (2009). *Where there are no dentists*. Berkeley, CA: Hesperian Health Guides.
Donlan, J. (2005). Health insurance exchange for employers: Interview with ConnectedHealth. Health Business Blog.
Durkheim, E. (1897/1951). *Suicide: A study in sociology*. New York: Free Press.
EFA Global Monitoring Report. (2013).
Freire, P. (1970). *Pedagogy of the oppressed*. 30th edition. Portland, OR: Bloomsbury Academic.
Hernandez-Murillo, R., & Martinek, C. J.. (2010, October). In some cases, a sick economy can be a prescription for good health. *The Regional Economist*. Federal Reserve Bank of St. Louis. http://www.stlouisfed.org/publications/re/articles/?id=2018.
Hernandez-Murillo, R., & Martinek, C. J. (2011, April). Which came first—Better education of better health? *The Regional Economist*. https://research.stlouisfed.org/publications/regional/11/04/health_education.pdf.
Himmelstein, D., Warren, E., Thorne, D., & Woolhandler, S. (2005, February). Marketwatch: Illness and injury as contributors to bankruptcy. *Health Affairs*, 2. doi:10.1377/hlthaff.w5.63.
Hitti, M. (2009, May 6). More education, better health. WebMD Health News. Reviewed by Louise Chang, MD. http://www.webmd.com/women/news/20090506/more-education-better-health.

Hoffmann, M. & Jensen, U. (2013). Does better education cause higher income? HWWI Research Paper 145.
Homann, M., & Jensen, U. (2013). *Does better education cause higher income?* Hamburg, Germany: Hamburg Institute of International Economics (HWWI), Research Paper, No. 145.
Klein, L. G., & Knitzer, J. (2007). Promoting effective early learning: What every policymaker and educator should know. National Center for Children in Poverty. http://nccp.org/publications/pdf/text_695.pdf.
Knee, J. A. (2015, August 26). The melting of Mark Zuckerberg's donation to Newark schools. *New York Times.*
Kohn, A. (1999). *Punished by rewards: The trouble with gold stars, incentive plans A's, praise, and other bribes.* Boston, MA: Houghton Mifflin.
Landry, S. H., Smith, K. E., & Miller-Loncar, C. I. (2000). Early maternal child influences on children's later independent and social functioning. *Child Development, 71,* 362–369.
Levy, B. S., & Sidel, V. W. (2005). *Social injustice and public health.* London: Oxford Scholarship.
Levy, B. S., & Sidel, V. W. (2013, November 9). Poverty and health in the United States. OUPblog. blog.oup.com/2013/N/poverty-public-health-united-states.
Mulvey, J. D., & Cooper, B. S. (2012). *Intersections of children's health, education and welfare.* New York: Palgrave Macmillan.
National Research Council and Institute of Medicine. (2004). *Children's health, the nation's wealth: Assessing and improving child health.* Washington, DC: The National Academics Press.
Nestvogel, R. (1995). *School education in 'third world' countries: Dream or trauma?* 205–215. https://www.waxmann.com/fileadmin/media/zusatztexte/postlethwaite/nestvoge.pdf.
New York Times. (1953, September 15). Education report: Horace Mann.
Nobel, K. G., Norman, M. F., & Farah, M. J. (2005, January). Neurocognitive correlates of socioeconomic status in kindergarten children. *Developmental Science, 8*(1), 74–87.
Obama, B. (2011). Speech delivered at Osawatomie High School in Kansas, December 6, 2011.
O'Neill, B., & Ensle, K. (2014). *Small Steps to Health and Wealth™*: Program Update and Research Insights. *The Forum for Family and Consumer Issues.* Raleigh, NC: North Carolina State University, Consortium.
Patil, N. (2012). Role of education social change. *International Educational E-Journal, 1*(2). *Science* (January 2011), *22*(1), 125–133.
Rowe, M., & Levine, R. (2009). Maternal literacy and child health in less developed countries: Evidence, processes and limitations. *Journal of Developmental & Behavioral Pediatrics, 30*(4), 340–349.
Russakoff, D. (2015). *The Prize.* New York: Random House.
Seward, B. L. (2006). *Managing stress: Principles and strategies for health and well-being* (5th ed.). Sudbury, MA: Jones and Bartlett.
Shinkman, R. (2015, April 27). Is there a link between financial and personal health? *Fierce Health Finance,* a division of Questex. http://www.fiercehealthfinance.com/story/there-link-between-financial-and-personal-health/2015-04-27.

Singer, A., & Pezone, M. (2003). Education for social change: From theory to practice. *Workplace, 5*(2), 145–151. http://louisville.edu/journal/workplace/issue5p2/singerpezone.html.

Snow, C. (2005, July/August). From literacy to learning. *Harvard Education Letter.* National Center for Children in Poverty.

Social Science Research Council. (2015). Health, education, and income: The basic building blocks of a good life. Measure of America.org. http://www.measureofamerica.org/health-education-and-income-the-basic-building-blocks-of-a-good-life/.

Sotomayor, S. (2013). *My Beloved World.* New York: Random House.

Thani, D. (2015). 20 best education systems in the world. MBC Times. www.mbctimes.com/english/20-best-education-systems-world.

Tucker-Drob, E. M., Briley, D, A., & Paige Harden, K. P. (2013, October). Genetic and environmental influences on cognition across development and context. *Curriculum Direction Psychology Sciences, 22*(5), 349–355.

US Census Bureau. (2014). Poverty. https://www.census.gov/www/poverty/about/overview/.

Voter Turnout Report. (2012). Bipartisan Policy Center. http://bipartisanpolicy.org/library/2012-voter-turnout/.

Werner, D., Maxwell, J., & Thurman, C. (2011). *Where there are no doctors: A village health care handbook.* Berkeley, CA: Hesperian Health Guides.

Index

Page indicators in italics indicate that a figure or table is being cited.

ability, 20, 99
academic performance: from behavioral difficulties, 27; from cognitive development, 55; expectation triad influence on, 18, *18*; learning influence on, 19; by mothers age, 29; readiness for, 57
achievement: of children, 21; by executive functions, 22; poverty influence on, 20–21; SES influence on, 15, *15*
agent of change, x
American Federation of Teachers, 83
asthma, 30

behavioral difficulties, 27
birth, 53, 55
brain development, 26, *26*, 27
brain matter, 26, *26*
Brown v. Board of Education, 97

career, 9
charter school, 52
childcare, 94, *94*
child development, 14–15, *15*
children: ability grouping of, 99; achievement of, 21; cognitive ability of, 21; educational support for, 77; education influence on, 34; environment of, 25–26; of foreign-born parent, 101; future of, 21; homeless trend of, 55; income influence on, 95; informal assessment of, 63; poverty of, 4, 13, 42; from teenage mothers, 29. *See also* early childhood education
citizenship, xii, 72
civic mindedness, 71
classroom, 44–45, 85
cognitive ability: of children, 21; environment influence on, 16, 61; particulate matter influence on, 31; stimulation for, 37
cognitive development: academic performance from, 55; factors for, xii, 116; health influence on, 36; life experiences for, 20; life success by, 14; poverty influence on, 14, 15; services for, 32; stress influence on, 91–92
cognitive skills: early enrollment for, 16; economics of, 22–23; learning experiences for, 16; productive abilities from, 16
Common Core State Standards, 43

community: application of, 82; classic definition of, 81; classroom as, 85; collaboration of, 82–83, 87; cultural understanding through, 72; definition of, 81; Dewey for, 6; disparity of, 58; early childhood education for, 35; education in, 81–82; environment of, 13; funding for, 115–16; improvement of, 13, 42, 71; internationality of, 105; key factors of, 86; leaders of, 77; national level of, 83; ownership of, 85; partnership through, 85; political support for, 71–72; programs for, 91; relationships of, 86, *86*; resources of, 52; for school, 88; state level of, 84–85; teacher influence on, 76
cortex development, 37
cultural understanding, 72
cultures, xi

deafness, 100
death rate, 110
democracy: citizenship for, xii; education for, 6, 10, 70, 120; investments for, 73
demographics, x–xi, 70
developmental milestones, 75
Dewey, John, 6
disability, 99, 100–101
Durkheim, Emile, 3

early childhood education: for community, 35; evidence for, 37; importance of, 74; for poverty, 78; for school, 35; subsidies for, 62; success from, 73–74; teacher of, 34
early enrollment, 16
early readiness principles, 28
economics: of cognitive skills, 22–23; disparity in, 58; education for, xi, 8; future of, 59; of life and death, 49

education. *See* specific topics
educational costs, 32
educational development: age of, xii; comparison of, 69; curricula for, 69; gap in, 15–16; hours for, 13–14; interconnection of, 42; intervention for, 35; language for, 25; philosophy on, 5; poverty influence on, 61; programs for, 32–33, *33*; ranking of, 13, 41; reform for, 36; steps for, 106; support for, 77; trajectory of, 114; trends from, 69
educational opportunity: harnessing of, 87; Kohn on, 4; Mann for, 10; relationship of, 106
educational quality: issues of, 41–42; SES on, 7, *7*; student influenced by, 47–48
Education for All (EFA), 5
Education for All Handicapped Children Act, 99
EFA. *See* Education for All
The Efficiency Index: Which Education Systems Deliver the Best Value for the Money, 41
Elementary and Secondary Education Act (ESEA), 87, 118
email exchange, 44–45
employment, 51, 108–9
environment: of childhood, 25–26; cognitive ability influenced by, 16, 61; of community, 13; conditions of, 3; fetal development from, 31; Lewontin on, 19–20; rebuilding of, 64; social mobility influenced by, 56; stress of, 74
equality: of living conditions, 106; politics of, 52; for poverty, 9
ESEA. *See* Elementary and Secondary Education Act
Every Student Succeeds Act, 76, 78
executive functions, 22
expectation triad, 18, *18*

family: childcare for, 94, *94*; education of, 48–49; in medical debt, 109; in poverty, 14; power of, 95–96; of student, 78
famous individuals, ix–x
fetal development, 31
foreign-born parent, 101
FPE. *See* Friends of Public Education
free market enterprise, 59–60
Freire, Paulo, 4, 5–6
Friends of Public Education (FPE), 88
funding: allocation of, 118; for community, 115–16; of government programs, 73; poverty influenced by, 115; for school, 72–73, 98–99

government: for free market enterprise, 59–60; funding by, 55, 73; policies of, 32
graduation: of high school, 46; rates of, 45–46, 51; by wealth, 56

hazardous waste, 31
health: cognitive development influenced by, 36; education influence on, 106, 112–13, 118; employment influence on, 108–9; from hazardous waste, 31; income influence on, 48, 49, 109–10, 113; for nation, 119; from nutrition, 53; policymaking for, 114; from poverty, 30, 57, *57*; by race, 113; school absence from, 30; SES influence on, 107–8, *108*, 110; wealth influence on, 48, 107, 119
healthy start, 63
higher education, 112
high school, 46
homelessness, 55, 58

immigrants, xi, 36
imprisonment, 51
income: children influenced by, 95; education influence on, 96, *96*, 110–11; health influenced by, 48, 49, 109–10, 113; inequality of, 60; life quality from, 48; math proficiency by, 53, *54*; opportunity influenced by, 53; raising of, 119–20; reading score by, 53, *54*; of school population, 52
inequality: facts of, 57–58; of income, 60; Obama on, x; prenatal care influence on, 53; by professionals, 70; protests for, 60, 71; social mobility influenced by, 58–59
infant, 35
informal assessment, 63
intergenerational experience: education for, 92–93, 102; five Ps of, 93; improvement of, xii; limits of, 101–2; policies for, 96–97
international education ranking, 41
in utero, 27

job opportunities, 112

knowledge: access to, 105; influence by, 3; vocabulary influence on, 22
Kohn, Alfie, 19

language, 25, 47
leaders, 77
learning: academic performance from, 19; brain development from, 26, *26*, 27; cognitive skills from, 16; developmental milestones of, 75; of language, 47; prerequisites for, 25; preventative measures for, xii; SES influence on, 62; standards for, 28
learning community, 86
learning strategy, 18–19
learning theory, 62
legislation changes, 88
Lewontin, Richard, 19–20
life: experiences of, 20; outcome of, 49; quality of, 48; stages of, 31; success in, 14
life and death, 49

lifespan, 114
living conditions, 106

Mann, Horace: common school by, 6, 114; on educational power, 10; philosophy of, 70
Maranganbassa, Antonio, 116–17
mastery goals, 18
mathematics: by Common Core State Standards, 43; income influence on, 53, *54*; international comparison of, 43; performance in, 33; by TEDS-M, 43, 46
medical debt, 109
Microsoft PowerPoint, 44
middle class, 94–95
mother's age, 29
multimedia presentations, 45

National Education Association, 83
nature or nurture, 56
negative stereotypes, 19
Nestvogel, Renate, 3–4
nutrition, 53

Obama, Barack, x
OECD. *See* Organisation for Economic Co-operation and Development
online, 44
opportunity, ix
oppression, 4
Organisation for Economic Co-operation and Development (OECD), 7, 7–8, 32, 58, 92

Pakistan girls, 3–4
parents: as disability advocate, 100–101; education of, 34, 92; influence of, 93; of poverty, 76; social mobility from, 28; technology influenced by, 93–94
particulate matter, 31
Patil, Namita, ix
performance categories, 18–19
personal growth, 18
personal stories, 8, 105

Pew Research Center, 36
PISA. *See* Programme for International Student Assessment
policymaking: for education, ix, xii; on educational costs, 32; for health, 114
political participation, 70–71
political support, 71–72
politics, 52
pollution, 30–31
poor education, 43–44
population, xii
Population and Development, 91
population growth, 5
Portugal, 7
poverty: ability influenced by, 20; achievement influenced by, 20–21; behavior from, 14; beliefs on, 59; birth influenced by, 53, 55; brain matter by, 26, *26*; breaking of, 61; children of, 4, 13, 42; cognitive development influenced by, 14, 15; conditions of, 56–57; early childhood education for, 78; educational development influenced by, 61; educational hours influenced by, 13–14; education for, 7, 10; EFA on, 5; equal opportunity for, 9; family in, 14; Freire on, 5; funding influence on, 115; hazardous waste of, 31; health from, 30, 57, *57*; history of, 51; hopelessness of, 60; language development influenced by, 25; motivation from, 61–62; negative consequences of, 19; parents of, 76; programs for, 63–64; reality of, 59; of school, 60; stress from, 22; studies on, 33–34; in utero conditions from, 27
power: of education, x, 116; of family, 95–96; Mann on, 10; of teacher union, 84
prenatal care: inequality influence by, 53; by SES, 28; teenage births influenced by, 28, *29*

preventative measures, xii
productive abilities, 16
professors, xii
profit, 74
Programme for International Student Assessment (PISA): countries ranking by, 33; educational ranking in, 13; on SES, 92
property value, 111
prosperity, 9–10
public school: change of, xii; demographics of, 70; failures of, 47, 69; political agenda of, 70; reinvention of, 77
publishing companies, 74–75

race, 55–56, 113
reactive-responding behavior, 17, *17*
reading score, 53, *54*
research community, 75
Roosevelt, Franklin Delano, 95
ruling class, 70

school: absence from, 30; clinics for, 35; cognitive skills from, 16; community for, 88; early childhood education for, 35; early readiness principles for, 28; external conditions of, 3; funding for, 72–73, 98–99; government funding for, 55; improvement of, 81; inequities of, 55; leaders of, 72; by Mann, 6, 114; population of, 52; poverty of, 60; profit influence on, 74; program for, 33; publishing companies for, 74–75; readiness for, 62–63; repair of, 73; segregation of, 97; selection of, 96; solutions for, 34; spending by, 111–12
School Education in "Third World" Countries: Dream or Trauma? (Nestvogel), 3–4
sciences, 46–47
segregation: of education, x; of school, 97; by wealth, 56

Serrano v. Priest, 98
SES. *See* socioeconomic status
Sherman, Richard: career of, 9; at Stanford University, 8; story of, 117
skilled labor, 92
socialized medicine, 107
social justice, 5–6
social mobility: education influence on, 115; environment influence on, 56; inequality influence on, 58–59; parenting for, 28; quintile of, 63; reasons for, ix
societal participation, 7
society: Durkheim on, 3; education for, xii; identification of, 4
socioeconomic status (SES): achievement by, 15, *15*; brain development from, 27; child development by, 14–15, *15*; disparities from, 62; educational gap by, 15–16; on educational quality, 7, *7*; executive functions by, 22; of famous individuals, ix–x; functioning by, 60–61; health influenced by, 107–8, *108*, 110; learning influenced by, 62; OECD on, 7, 7–8; performance comparison by, 30; PISA on, 92; prenatal care by, 28; quality by, 7, *7*; reactive-responding influenced by, 17, *17*; resources for, 98; work ethic by, 9
Sotomayor, Sonia, 9, 117
specialized education, 98
standardize tests, 47
Stanford University, 8
stress: cognitive development influenced by, 91–92; of environment, 74; from poverty, 22
student: educational quality influence on, 47–48; family of, 78; negative stereotypes of, 19; OECD on, 32; Singer and Pezone on, 19; work published of, 45

teacher: community influenced by, 76; of early childhood education, 34; education from, 43–44; education of, 75, 78; influence of, 88; quality of, 33, 35–36; training of, 34, 76; treatment of, 117
Teacher Education Study in Mathematics (TEDS-M), 46
teacher union: by American Federation of Teachers, 83; influence of, 87; merger of, 84; by National Education Association, 83; power of, 84; roles of, 83–84
technology, 44, 93–94
TEDS-M. *See* Teacher Education Study in Mathematics

teenage births, 28, *29*
teenage mothers, 28–29
teenage pregnancy, 29
Title I grants, 63
trade skill, 119

universal education, 106–7

voter representation, 114

wealth: health influenced by, 48, 107, 119; segregation by, 56
webquest, 44
welfare, 118
work ethic, 9

About the Authors

Janet D. Mulvey, PhD, is program director, TARA Center OASIS College Support Program, and assistant professor, educational leadership, at Pace University, New York City, with a focus on research and improving public schooling. Publications include *Schools Affected by the Financial Crisis*: The Doyle Report Online (2008); *Feminization of Schools:* the School Administrator (AASA), September 2009; *Getting and Keeping New Teachers: Six Essentials Steps from Recruitment to Retention* (Rowman & Littlefield Publishers, 2009); *Blurring the Lines: Charter, Public, Private and Religious Schools Come Together* (2010); "Faith Based Charter Schools: Debate," in *Faith Based Schools* (2011); "Faith Based Charter Schools," in *Praeger Handbook of Faith-Based Schools in the United States, K–12*, volume I (2011); "Should Faith-Based Charter School Survive Constitutional Scrutiny?" in *Alternative Schooling and School Choice* (2012); *Intersections of Children's Health, Education and Welfare* (2012); *Education Is Special for Everyone* (Rowman & Littlefield, 2014); and "Connecting Education, Welfare and Health for American Families," in *Peabody Journal of Education* (2015).

Bruce S. Cooper, PhD, is professor emeritus at Fordham University, Graduate School of Education, with a focus on research including (1) politics and policy in education with books, *Better Policies, Better Schools, Handbook of Education Politics and Policy*; (2) in private school religious education, with his book *Blurring the Lines*, and "Finding a Golden Mean in Education Policy: Centering Religious and Public Schools," in the *Peabody Journal of Education*; and (3) fixing school problems, with books *Fixing Truancy Now*, with Jon Shute; *Truancy Revisited* with Rita Guare; and *Mentoring with Meaning* with Carlos McCray.

www.ingramcontent.com/pod-product-compliance
Lightning Source LLC
Chambersburg PA
CBHW021525240426
43669CB00041BA/137